To Mr Bernard H. Einarson

With Thanks

The Lindsay Curling Club

1988

THE RIVER CLASS DESTROYERS
of the Royal Canadian Navy

Ken Macpherson

Foreword by Com. James Plomer, RCN (ret'd.)

And Associates, Publishers Toronto

First published 1985
by Charles J. Musson and Associates, Publishers
P.O. Box 686, Station "Q", Toronto, Ontario.

©1985 by Kenneth R. Macpherson

All rights reserved. No part of this publication may be reproduced, stored in a retrieval system, or transmitted in any form or by any means, electronic, mechanical, photocopying, recording, or otherwise, without prior written permission of the publisher.

Canadian Cataloguing in Publication Data

Macpherson, Ken.
   The river class destroyers of the Royal Canadian Navy

Bibliography: p.
ISBN 0-920845-00-2

1. Destroyers (Warships) – Canadian – History –
20th century. 2. Canada. Royal Canadian Navy –
Lists of vessels. I. Title.

V825.5.C3M26 1985   623.8'254'0971   C85-098990-6

CONTENTS

Foreword   7
Preface   9
HMCS *Saguenay*   11
HMCS *Skeena*   18
HMCS *Fraser*   26
HMCS *St. Laurent*   30
HMCS *Ottawa*   37
HMCS *Restigouche*   47
HMCS *Assiniboine*   53
HMCS *Margaree*   62
HMCS *Ottawa* (2nd)   63
HMCS *Kootenay*   68
HMCS *Saskatchewan*   74
HMCS *Gatineau*   82
HMCS *Chaudière*   87
HMCS *Qu'Appelle*   92
General Notes   97
Internal Arrangement Diagram   98-99
Particulars of the River Class   100-101
Explanatory Notes   102
Selected Bibliography   102
Photograph Credits   103

FOREWORD

As opposed to hand-me-downs, the first brand new destroyers we ever owned were the "River" class H.M.C.S. *Skeena* and *Saguenay*. With certain Canadian modifications these were copies of the Royal Navy's successful new "A" class flotilla. Delivered in 1931 when our naval forces were at a particularly low ebb, this was an historic event.

Yarrow's yard in Equimalt, so one was told on good authority, claimed that with more time they could build them. What their costs would have been is not known, but whatever the reason, the contract went overseas to Thornycroft's yard in Southampton. They proved to be fine ships.

As a member of the pre-war R.C.N.V.R. it was my good fortune to serve in *Skeena* for three months in the early part of that eventful year 1939. In command was H.T.W. Grant, one of our ablest sea-captains from whom one was able to learn much.

This was an eventful cruise. We met the four later "River" class acquisitions from the west coast: *Ottawa, Fraser, Restigouche* and *St. Laurent*, in Jamaica, at that time the biggest congregation of Canadian warships ever. Steaming to Bermuda we joined up with five of H.M. cruisers to take part in an extended exercise, an attempt to cut off an "enemy" raider, under the command of Commodore H. Harwood. Less than a year later, with *Exeter* and *Ajax* from this squadron and the addition of *Achilles*, he would end the career of the pocket battleship *Admiral Graf Spee* in the Battle of the River Plate.

Even identical sister ships have their individual personalities. Each in a different way would become a victim of the war. As you will also discover in these interesting pages they had a number of successors with remarkable variety in their lives.

James Plomer
Commodore, RCN (ret'd)

PREFACE

The self-propelled torpedo and the torpedo boat to deliver it had, by the mid-1880s, reached a point of development that made a counter-measure imperative, and in 1894 the Royal Navy commissioned its first "torpedo boat destroyer". As the name makes clear, its function was to defend larger fleet units against attack by torpedo boats, and to this end its own armament included three torpedo tubes.

HMS *Havock* marked the beginning of an evolutionary process that, by 1930, had produced a craft of more than five times her displacement, armed with four 4.7" guns and eight torpedo tubes. These latter-day destroyers also carried depth charges with which to attack submerged submarines, but their proper function was still considered to be that of screening the fleet. The 1939-45 war was to change all that and see most of them, like thoroughbreds in harness, cast in the plodding role of watchdog to trade convoys.

When Canada entered the Second World War on September 10, 1939, her entire offensive naval force consisted of six destroyers. All being named for Canadian rivers, they came to be known semi-officially as the River class although not all, properly speaking, were sister-ships.

Saguenay and *Skeena* had been commissioned in 1931, the first fighting vessels ever built to Canadian order. *Fraser*, *St. Laurent*, *Ottawa* and *Restigouche* were acquired 1937-38, all of them units of the Royal Navy's "C" class. With the commissioning of *Assiniboine*, the flotilla-leader of the same class, in October 1939, the entire half-flotilla was now in RCN service.

Three "Rivers" enjoy a brief respite between convoys at "Newfiejohn" in mid-1942. Ottawa (left) and Saguenay (right) became casualties later that year, and Skeena in 1944.

Fraser, lost in the evacuation of France in 1940, was replaced by *Margaree*, a former RN "D" class ship which, sadly, was herself lost within a few weeks of commissioning. *Ottawa* was torpedoed and sunk in September 1942, and *Saguenay* permanently disabled two months later.

Shortage of destroyers in Canadian escort groups thus led to the Admiralty's releasing six of its older destroyers, and these were commissioned in the RCN between March 1943 and February 1944. Variously members of the "D", "E", "F", "G" and "H" classes, they also became members of the River class and were renamed accordingly: *Chaudière, Gatineau, Kootenay, Ottawa* (2nd), *Qu'Appelle* and *Saskatchewan*.

The Rivers were not old ships by ordinary standards, but wartime demands aged them rapidly, and they did not survive to serve in the postwar Navy. A new generation of ships has borne their names and battle honours, recalling with pride the large contribution made by these fourteen hard-worked ships to the cause of victory in the Second World War.

I acknowledge with gratitude once again the assistance of Dr. W.A.B. Douglas, Head of the Directorate of History, NDHQ, and his staff, particularly David Kealy and Marc Milner; and the individuals listed on page 103, through whose kindness a good many hitherto unpublished photographs appear in this book. Among them is James Plomer, who did me the further kindness of writing the Foreword.

Special thanks, finally, to my friend and fellow naval enthusiast, John Burgess, for permission to reproduce his laboriously compiled "Daily State" resumés.

SAGUENAY

The first made-to-order RCN warship, *Saguenay* was commissioned on May 22, 1931, at Portsmouth, England. In company with *Skeena*, she sailed for Halifax on June 25 and on July 3 made her way up the harbour to an enthusiastic welcome. That September she steamed up the river for which she was named, and visited Chicoutimi.

With *Champlain,* a much older destroyer transferred to the RCN in 1929, *Saguenay* made up the Eastern Division of Canada's infant Navy, and the two took part in the Jacques Cartier Quatercentenary celebration at Gaspé in August 1934. That January they had called at Bermuda, Jamaica and Colón, where *Skeena* and *Vancouver*

(1) Saguenay in 1931, brand new.

(2) Saguenay in the mid-1930s. Pendant number H01 was reassigned in 1936 to HMS Hotspur.

(3) Saguenay on a visit to Montreal, August 21, 1934.

(*Champlain's* sister-ship) joined them, having come round from Esquimalt. The four then proceeded on a grand tour of Caribbean ports. In the course of this cruise they exercised with ships of the Home Fleet, among them the "C" class half-flotilla, which was to join the RCN a few years later.

In the summer of 1936 *Saguenay* escorted Great War veterans on their pilgrimage to Vimy Ridge for the

(4) *Saguenay on Caribbean exercises early in 1939.*

(5) *Saguenay in October 1940, unchanged as yet except for her pendant number, "I" superior instead of "D".*

dedication of the Vimy Memorial. The following year *Skeena* was transferred to the east coast, and on May 20 she and *Saguenay* represented Canada at King George VI's coronation review. On May 15, 1939, the two met S.S. *Empress of Australia,* bringing the King and Queen for a tour of Canada, and escorted the liner up the St. Lawrence to Quebec City. At the end of the tour a month later, they saw the royal couple some distance to sea, a function very soon to be known as that of "local escort".

On September 10, 1939, Canada declared war on Germany, and six days later *Saguenay* and *St. Laurent* escorted the inaugural convoy, HX.1. Later that month *Saguenay* was assigned to the America & West Indies Station, based on Kingston, Jamaica, and on October 23 intercepted the German tanker *Emmy Friederich* in

(6) Saguenay in Hvalfjord, Iceland, August 1941, after escorting HMS Prince of Wales that far. The battleship had on board Sir Winston Churchill, homebound from the Atlantic Charter meeting in Placentia Bay, Newfoundland. The "dazzle paint" is typical for the period.

(7) Saguenay in mid-1942, with the earlier wartime modifications all in place: shortened after funnel; mainmast removed; "Y" gun gone from the quarterdeck; 3" H.A. gun in place of the after torpedo tubes; and Type 296M RDF antenna at the masthead.

(8) Saguenay after losing her stern on November 15, 1942, in collision with a merchant ship. Since the photo on page 14 was taken, she had acquired a Type 271 RDF set.

(9) Saguenay at St. John's, November 18, 1942, with her wardroom laid open to the sea.

Yucatan Channel. The tanker's crew scuttled her.

At the end of November *Saguenay* returned to Halifax, resuming local escort duties until October 16, 1940, when she sailed for Britain to join EG 10, Greenock. En route she rescued 32 survivors of S.S. *Cubano* and *Sulaco*, torpedoed in convoy OB.229. On December 1, 1940, while escorting convoy HG.47 northward from Gibraltar, *Saguenay* was torpedoed by the Italian submarine *Argo*, some 300 miles west of Ireland. With her bows wrecked and 21 of her ship's company dead, she managed to struggle under her own power nearly all the way to Barrow-in-Furness, arriving on December 5.

Saguenay's repairs were not completed until May 22, 1941, just in time for her to help screen major units of the Home Fleet as far as Iceland in their hunt for the *Bismarck*. Recalled to Newfoundland to become part of the Newfoundland Escort Force then forming there, *Saguenay* arrived at St.

John's on June 7. The following month she had the privilege of escorting HMS *Prince of Wales* as far as Iceland, the battleship having on board Winston Churchill, homebound from his conference at Placentia Bay with President Roosevelt.

As escort to convoy ON.52 in January 1942, *Saguenay* suffered storm damage so severe that she barely reached St. John's, and three months' work was needed to make her seaworthy again. When she resumed service on the "Newfie-Derry" run, it was as a member of the newly designated EG C-3, based on Londonderry.

On November 15, 1942, *Saguenay* was involved in a collision with the Panamanian freighter *Azra* south of Cape Race, Nfld., losing her stern. The freighter was sunk by the explosion of the destroyer's depth charges, but the ships suffered only two fatalities between them. *Saguenay* was towed to St. John's, where it was decided to convert her to a stationary training ship. Her abbreviated stern was accordingly sealed off, and she was taken in October 1943 to spend the remainder of the war as a tender to HMCS Cornwallis. Paid off on July 30, 1945, she was broken up in 1946 by International Iron & Metal Co., Hamilton.

(10) Saguenay at the yard of the Saint John Shipbuilding Co., March 31, 1943. She was there until the end of July, being fitted as a stationary training ship.

(11) Saguenay at Cornwallis in 1944, her truncated stern quite obvious. "A" gun had been removed since the photo above was taken.

D/S DATE	GROUP, etc.	STATUS	D/S DATE	GROUP, etc.	STATUS	D/S DATE	GROUP, etc.	STATUS
Mar. 2/42	Mid-Ocean Escort	Repairs, Saint John, N.B.	Dec. 22/42	MOEF	Left in tow for Halifax, Dec. 21	Dec. 7/43	Training Duties, Admin. by Halifax	Moored Training Ship at Digby, N.S.
Mar. 10/42	"	"	Dec. 31/42	"	Arrived in tow from Halifax at Saint John, Dec. 30	Dec. 21/43	Trg. Duties Admin. by "Cornwallis"	"
Mar. 20/42	"	"	Jan. 8/43	"	At Saint John for refit	Jan. 11/44	"	"
Apr. 2/42	"	"	Jan. 14/43	"	"	Jan. 25/44	"	"
Apr. 10/42	"	"	Feb. 4/43	"	"	Feb. 8/44	"	"
Apr. 21/42	"	SC.79	Feb. 13/43	-	"	Feb. 22/44	"	"
May 1/42	"	Londonderry	Feb. 23/43	-	"	Mar. 7/44	"	"
May 11/42	"	ON.93	Mar. 2/43	-	"	Mar. 21/44	"	"
May 21/42	"	St. John's	Mar. 10/43	Decommissioned	"	Apr. 11/44	"	"
June 2/42	MOEF	HX.191	Mar. 23/43	"	"	Apr. 25/44	"	"
June 11/42	"	Arr. Londonderry, June 5	Apr. 1/43	Paid off for long repairs	"	May 9/44	"	"
June 22/42	"	ON.104	Apr. 14/43	"	"	May 23/44	"	"
July 2/42	"	Arr. St. John's, June 27	Apr. 27/43	"	"	June 6/44	"	"
July 11/42	"	SC.90	May 3/43	"	"	June 20/44	"	"
July 22/42	"	Arr. Londonderry, July 15	May 13/43	"	"	July 4/44	"	"
Aug. 1/42	"	ON.115	May 22/43	"	"	July 18/44	"	"
Aug. 11/42	"	Arr. St. John's, Aug. 2	June 2/43	"	"	Aug. 8/44	"	Repairs, Saint John, N.B.
Aug. 22/42	"	En route to St. John's from ON.121	June 12/43	"	"	Aug. 22/44	"	Moored Training Ship at Digby, N.S.
Sep. 1/42	"	Arr. St. John's, Aug. 23	June 22/43	"	"	Sep. 5/44	"	"
Sep. 11/42	"	SC.98	July 6/43	"	"	Sep. 19/44	"	"
Sep. 22/42	"	ON.131	July 20/43	"	"	Oct. 3/44	"	"
Oct. 1/42	"	Arr. St. John's, Sept. 28	Aug. 3/43	Training Duties, Admin. by Halifax	"	Oct. 24/44	"	"
Oct. 12/42	"	HX.210	Aug. 17/43	"	Arrived at "Cornwallis" in tow, July 29	Nov. 7/44	"	"
Oct. 22/42	"	Arr. Londonderry, Oct. 15	Sep. 7/43	"	Moored Training ship at Digby, N.S.	Nov. 21/44	"	"
Nov. 2/42	"	ON.141	Sep. 21/43	"	"	Dec. 5/44	"	"
Nov. 11/42	"	Arr. Halifax Nov. 4; Repairs thero Nov. 5-13	Oct. 5/43	"	"	Dec. 19/44	"	"
Nov. 20/42	"	In collision Nov. 15; Arr. St. John's, Nov. 16	Oct. 19/43	"	"	Jan. 9/45	"	"
Dec. 2/42	"	St. John's	Nov. 9/43	"	"	Jan. 23/45	"	"
Dec. 12/42	"	"	Nov. 23/43	-	"	Feb. 6/45	"	"

See note on p.102

SAGUENAY

SKEENA

Second of Canada's tailor-made ships, *Skeena* was commissioned at Portsmouth, England, on June 10, 1931, a couple of weeks after her sister, *Saguenay*, and the two sailed for Canada on June 23. Five days after their maiden arrival at Halifax on July 3, *Skeena* set out for Esquimalt where, with the older destroyer *Vancouver*, she was to form the Western Division of the RCN.

On her first winter cruise, in January 1932, *Skeena* was involved in an unusual incident: on January 22, when en route to the Canal Zone, she was diverted to Acajutla, San Salvador, where a revolt seemed likely to endanger the lives of a number of British nationals. *Skeena's* armed shore party proved unnecessary, but she played host to some of the Britishers for a time before sailing for home.

With *Saguenay*, *Skeena* represented Canada at King George VI's coronation naval review on May 20, 1937, and a year later arrived at Halifax, having been replaced on the west coast by the newly-acquired *Fraser*. Among her last peacetime duties was the pleasant one of conveying the King and Queen from Cape Tormentine, N.B. to Charlottetown and thence to Pictou, during their Canadian tour in June 1939.

Skeena was at Halifax on September 3, 1939, when the war broke out, and the following day she embarked the

(12) Canada's first tailor-made warships arrived at Halifax, July 3, 1931. The photo was probably taken from Skeena. *At right is HMCS* Champlain, *who met them with Com. Walter Hose, Chief of Naval Staff, aboard.*

(13) Skeena at Bermuda in the 1930s, acting as a Commodore's flagship.

(14) Skeena at New York in June 1939, during the World's Fair.

Commander-in-Chief, America & West Indies Station, and his staff for passage to Bermuda. She returned to Halifax on September 11, the day after Canada declared war, to become the second member of Halifax Force. The Force was further augmented in mid-September by the arrival of *Fraser* and *St. Laurent* and, in December, *Ottawa* and *Restigouche*, all from the west coast. The six were chiefly employed as local escorts for HX and HXF convoys until late in May 1940 when four of them, *Skeena* included, were dispatched to the United Kingdom. Attached to Western Approaches Command, she was initially based on Plymouth but transferred in July to the Northern Escort Force at Rosyth. Later based on Greenock, Liverpool and Londonderry, she spent that summer and fall on escort, anti-submarine and convoy rescue duty. In the course of one of the latter missions, she took off 230 survivors of the torpedoed armed merchant cruiser *Cheshire,* then put aboard a steaming party which kept the crippled ship underway for several hours until salvage tugs took over.

In March 1941 *Skeena* returned to Halifax to refit, joining the recently formed Newfoundland Escort Force when the work was completed in June. The U-boat war was now in full swing, and *Skeena's* first experience with a wolf-pack action came that September, when she was escorting convoy SC.42 as Senior Officer of EG 24. The convoy

was attacked by 17 U-boats, who sank 16 merchant ships against the loss of two of their own. It was corvettes *Chambly* and *Moose Jaw* who made this the occasion of the RCN's first kill, sinking *U 501* on September 10.

Skeena's turn came in July 1942, when she was with convoy ON.115 as a member of Task Unit 4.1.13 (later designated C-3). The Senior Officer was in *Saguenay* and the rest of the group consisted of four corvettes. On July 31 *Skeena* and *Wetaskiwin* teamed up in a textbook attack that destroyed *U 588*.

Skeena was docked at Halifax on December 30 for a much-needed refit, rejoining C-3 at Londonderry in April 1943. For the better part of the succeeding year she endured the North Atlantic grind before again docking at Halifax for refit in February 1944. Crossing in April with SC.157, she joined Support Group EG 12 at 'Derry. Made up of *Skeena, Qu'Appelle, Restigouche, Assiniboine* and *Saskatchewan,* this "all-River" group had the task of screening Channel traffic from U-boat attack in the forthcoming invasion of Normandy.

EG 12 saw little excitement during June, but early in July took part in Operation "Dredger", a successful attack on a group of surface vessels escorting U-boats out of Brest. Fourteen of *Skeena's* crew were wounded, three seriously. An attack by the Luftwaffe on July 24 provided further drama, *Skeena* being near-missed by both conventional and glider bombs.

On August 12 the group carried out Operation "Kinetic", a successful strike against German ships attempting to

(15) Skeena at Plymouth, England, on June 2, 1940.

*(16) Canadian destroyers at Plymouth on June 2, 1950. **Skeena** is nearest, with **St. Laurent** alongside and **Restigouche** astern. Note ensigns flown at the yard.*

(17) Skeena arriving at Plymouth on May 31, 1940.

(18) Skeena in January 1942. Early wartime modifications include: pendant "I" superior instead of "D"; shortened after funnel; "Y" gun and mainmast removed; after torpedo tubes replaced by 3" H.A. gun; and Type 286M RDF antenna at the masthead.

supply a beleaguered German garrison in Audierne Bay. Toward the end of the fight *Skeena* collided with *Qu'Appelle* and was under repair for some weeks.

In September she joined EG 11 with *St. Laurent, Assiniboine, Qu'Appelle* and *Chaudière*. The new group was detailed to hunt for U-boats on passage to and from Norway, and on the night of October 24 they took refuge in Reykjavik harbour from gale-force winds. About 0200 the following morning *Skeena* dragged her anchors and was driven onto the rocks of Videy Island. An initial attempt to reach shore by Carley float resulted in the loss of fifteen men, fourteen of whose bodies were recovered and interred in Fossaburg cemetery. The remainder of the ship's company were rescued but the ship was adjudged a constructive total loss. Her remains were sold in June 1945 to an Icelandic resident, who salved her for scrap.

(19) Later changes to *Skeena* are evident in this view from the bridge, notably the new port-side 20mm gun platforms. Her forefunnel bears the badge of C-3 Escort Group. The photo was taken on April 8, 1944, shortly before her departure for D Day duties.

▲ (20) *Skeena* in D Day period camouflage, mid-1944.

▼ (21) *Skeena* wrecked on Videy Island, near Reykjavik, with salvage craft alongside, October 1944. Changes in armament show to good advantage.

D/S DATE	GROUP, etc.	STATUS	D/S DATE	GROUP, etc.	STATUS	D/S DATE	GROUP, etc	STATUS
Mar. 2/42	Mid-Ocean Escort	Repairs, Saint John, N.B.	Dec. 22/42	MOEF	Arrived St. John's Dec. 21	Dec. 7/43	EG C-3, MOEF	U.K.
Mar. 10/42	"	"	Dec. 31/42	"	Arrived Halifax Dec. 26	Dec. 21/43	"	Left U.K. Dec. 17 for ON.216
Mar. 20/42	"	"	Jan. 8/43	"	Refitting, Halifax	Jan. 11/44	"	Left St. John's Jan. 9 for Londonderry
Apr. 2/42	"	"	Jan. 14/43	"	"	Jan. 25/44	"	U.K.
Apr. 10/42	"	"	Feb. 4/43	"	"	Feb. 8/44	"	Left U.K. Jan. 29 c̄ ONS.28
Apr. 21/42	"	SC.79	Feb. 13/43	"	"	Feb. 22/44	"	Refitting, Halifax
May 1/42	"	Londonderry	Feb. 23/43	"	"	Mar. 7/44	"	Refitting, Shelburne
May 11/42	"	ON.93	Mar. 2/43	"	"	Mar. 21/44	"	"
May 21/42	"	St. John's	Mar. 10/43	"	"	Apr. 11/44	"	Arrived Halifax Apr. 6 from Shelburne
June 2/42	MOEF	HX.191	Mar. 23/43	"	"	Apr. 25/44	"	Left St. John's Apr. 23 for Londonderry
June 11/42	"	Arrived Londonderry June 5	Apr. 1/43	"	Completed Mar. 30: Ready for sea Apr. 8	May 9/44	12th EG, CiC - WAC	Londonderry
June 22/42	"	ON.104	Apr. 14/43	"	HX.233. (To A-3, then C-3)	May 23/44	12th EG, RCN	"
July 2/42	"	Arrived St. John's June 27	Apr. 27/43	EG C-3, MOEF	Arrived U.K. Apr. 27	June 6/44	"	Plymouth
July 11/42	"	SC.90	May 3/43	"	ON.180	June 20/44	"	At sea
July 21/42	"	Arrived Londonderry July 15	May 13/43	"	Arrived St. John's May 8	July 4/44	"	At sea
Aug. 1/42	"	En route St. John's from ON.115	May 22/43	"	HX.238	July 18/44	"	At sea
Aug. 11/42	"	Arrived St. John's Aug. 2	June 2/43	"	U.K.	Aug. 8/44	"	Londonderry
Aug. 22/42	"	En route St. John's from ON.121	June 12/43	"	Arrived St. John's June 10	Aug. 22/44	12th EG, CiC - WAC	Plymouth
Sep. 1/42	"	Arrived St. John's Aug. 23	June 22/43	EG C-4, MOEF	HX.244	Sep. 5/44	"	"
Sep. 11/42	"	SC.98	July 6/43	"	Arrived U.K. from HX.244 (temporarily in C-3)	Sep. 19/44	11th EG, CiC - WAC	Repairs, Plymouth
Sep. 22/42	"	ON.131	July 20/43	EG C-3, MOEF	Arrived St. John's July 18 from ON.192	Oct. 3/44	"	At sea
Oct. 1/42	"	Arrived St. John's Sep. 28	Aug. 3/43	"	Left St. John's July to join HX.249	Oct. 24/44	11th EG, CiC - Plymouth	At sea
Oct. 12/42	"	HX.210	Aug. 17/43	"	U.K.	Nov. 7/44	NWAC, unallocated	Wrecked at Reykjavik Oct.25
Oct. 22/42	"	Arrived Londonderry Oct. 15	Sep. 7/43	"	Left Halifax Sep.5 for St. John's	Nov. 21/44		
Nov. 2/42	"	En route U.K. from ON.141	Sep. 21/43	"	U.K.	Dec. 5/44		
Nov. 11/42	"	Arrived St. John's Nov. 5	Oct. 5/43	"	Left U.K. Sep. 27 c̄ ONS.19	Dec. 19/44		
Nov. 20/42	"	SC.109	Oct. 19/43	"	Left St. John's Oct. 16 for HX.261	Jan. 9/45		
Dec. 2/42	"	Arrived Iceland Nov. 25	Nov. 9/43	"	U.K.	Jan. 23/45		
Dec. 12/42	"	ONS.152	Nov. 23/43	"	Left St. John's Nov. 22 for SC.147	Feb. 6/45		

See note on p.102

SKEENA

FRASER

Launched as HMS *Crescent* on September 29, 1931, she served with the 2nd Destroyer Flotilla of the Home Fleet until September 9, 1936, when she was paid off to refit for transfer to the RCN. On February 17, 1937, she was commissioned at Chatham as HMCS *Fraser*. Her sister, HMS *Cygnet*, was commissioned on the same occasion, becoming HMCS *St. Laurent.*

The two left Portland on March 12 for Barbados, visiting the Azores en route, and arrived at their destination on March 24 to find *Skeena* and *Saguenay* awaiting them. *Skeena* and *Fraser* exchanged commanding officers and *Fraser* set out alone for Esquimalt, transiting the Panama Canal early in April. She arrived at Esquimalt on May 3, and for the rest of the year carried out training while making courtesy visits to a number of British Columbia communities. She also embarked the Governor-General, Lord Tweedsmuir,

▲ *(22) HMS Crescent, who became HMCS Fraser in 1937.*

▼ *(23) Fraser off the B.C. coast, 1937-39.*

for his visit to the B.C. mainland, and in September was part of the escort when President Roosevelt visited the province.

The end of January 1938 found all four "Rivers" together on a cruise that took them to the Galapagos Islands and to a number of Peruvian and Costa Rican ports. En route north, several Mexican ports received visits, as did San Diego. The rest of the year was spent in home waters, in the familiar dual role of training and visiting.

The 1939 winter cruise took *Fraser* farther afield. Accompanied by *St. Laurent* and the recently acquired *Ottawa* and *Restigouche*, she sailed on January 24 for Jamaica. There they joined *Saguenay* and *Skeena* for exercises with cruisers of the Home Fleet. The four west coast destroyers were back at Esquimalt on April 28, and late the following month escorted the King and Queen from Vancouver to Victoria and back.

A visit of the four destroyers to Vancouver in connection with the Canadian Pacific Exhibition was rudely interrupted on August 31, when *Fraser* and *St. Laurent* were abruptly ordered to Halifax. They were on their way less than two hours later, and were passing through the Panama Canal when word was received that Canada was at war with Germany. *Fraser* arrived at Halifax on September 14, and five days later, with *Saguenay* and *Skeena*, carried out her first stint as a local escort with convoy HXF.1. In October she escorted into Halifax a Royal Navy

(24) Fraser off the B.C. coast, 1937-39.

◀ *(25) Fraser off the B.C. coast, July 4, 1938.*

(26) **Fraser** transiting the Panama Canal in April 1937. The autographs are those of her C.O., Cdr. H.E. Reid, and other officers.

squadron carrying gold bullion from the Bank of England for safekeeping in Canada, and late that month performed the same service for HMS *Ascania*, similarly laden. On November 14 *Fraser* was in collision with the trawler HMCS *Bras d'Or*, and was under repair until December 4. On the 10th she was one of four destroyers that sailed as local escort to TC.1, a troop convoy of five large liners carrying the First Canadian Division to England.

In March 1940 *Fraser* was detached to join the Jamaica Force patrolling the Caribbean, and arrived at Kingston, Jamaica, on the 31st. For the next two months she was kept very busy intercepting and investigating foreign merchant ships, but on May 26 she left Bermuda for the U.K., and a week later was in Plymouth. After a two-week refit she became Senior Officer of the small group of Canadian destroyers now in British waters.

On June 21, with France on the verge of collapse, *Fraser* and *Restigouche* were ordered to assist in the evacuation of St. Jean de Luz, a small port near the Spanish border. This operation was largely complete by the 25th when the French surrendered, and the Canadian destroyers stood out from the harbour with the cruiser HMS *Calcutta*, bound for England.

Late that evening, a misunderstanding of signals between *Fraser* and *Calcutta* led to the cruiser's ramming *Fraser*, cutting her in two just ahead of the bridge. Forty-five of *Fraser's* ship's company were lost, the rest being rescued by *Calcutta* and *Restigouche*. *Fraser's* bow section sank fairly quickly, but her after part had to be re-boarded and scuttled. Ironically, most of her survivors were lost in the sinking of HMCS *Margaree*, again by ramming, four months later.

▲ *(27) Fraser on exercises in the Caribbean, 1939.*

(28) Fraser off St. Jean de Luz during the evacuation of France, June 25, 1940. She was accidentally lost that evening. The photo was taken from the freighter **Baron Nairn**.

ST. LAURENT

Launched on September 29, 1931, as HMS *Cygnet*, she served with the 2nd Destroyer Flotilla of the Home Fleet until Spetember 30, 1936, when she was paid off to refit for transfer to the RCN. Her recommissioning as HMCS *St. Laurent* took place on February 17, 1937, at Chatham, *Fraser* being commissioned on the same occasion.

The two sailed for Barbados on March 12 via the Azores, where they were to refuel. They arrived on the 24th at Barbados, where *Saguenay* and *Skeena* were waiting for them. *Fraser* then proceeded alone to Esquimalt and the others to Halifax, where they arrived on April 8. In May, *St. Laurent* sailed up the river whose name she bore and visited Montreal for five days, afterward calling at Quebec City and Chicoutimi. The summer was spent in a busy round of courtesy visits to Maritime ports.

It was decided in 1938 that *Skeena*, who had since returned to the west coast, should exchange stations with *St. Laurent*, so as to have two identical ships on each coast. This was done following exercises in the Pacific, and *St. Laurent* and *Fraser* spent the rest of the summer together in B.C. waters, training. Late that year they were joined on the west coast by their recently acquired sisters, *Ottawa* and *Restigouche*, and early in 1939 the four joined *Saguenay* and *Skeena* in West Indian waters for a winter cruise.

(29) HMS Cygnet *in 1932. She became HMCS* St. Laurent *in 1937.*

▶ *(30) St. Laurent on exercises in the Caribbean early in 1939.*

(31) St. Laurent off Saint John, N.B., 1938.

At the end of May the four west-coast "Rivers" had the honour of escorting the King and Queen from Vancouver to Victoria and back. That August they were all at Vancouver, taking part in the Canadian Pacific Exhibition, when, owing to the worsening international situation, *Fraser* and *St. Laurent* were ordered to Halifax. They left precipitately, and were transiting the Panama Canal when war was declared by Canada on September 10.

The two fuelled at Kingston, Jamaica, then sailed for Halifax, where *St. Laurent* arrived on September 15. She commenced wartime operation the very next day, as local escort to the first of the HX convoys. With *Fraser*, on October 15, she screened the "Detached Squadron" carrying bullion from the Bank of England, and on November 6 escorted HMS *Ascania* into Halifax with a further £2 million aboard. In December, *St. Laurent* and the other three Halifax-based Rivers served as local escort to convoy TC.1, carrying 7,400 men of the First Canadian Division to Britain.

With the fall of France imminent, the four destroyers were ordered in May 1940 to proceed to the U.K. *St. Laurent* and *Restigouche* assisted on June 11 in efforts to evacuate troops from the French coast in the vicinity of Le Havre. *St. Laurent* was then put to general use by Western Approaches Command on escort and anti-submarine patrol. On July 2 she went to the assistance of M.V. *Arandora Star*, torpedoed northwest of Ireland. She succeeded in rescuing some 850 of the passengers, German and Italian internees or prisoners-of-war. Crewmen were also rescued from S.S. *Titan*, September 4, and S.S. *Conch*, December 1. Late that day *St. Laurent* and HMS *Viscount* picked up all survivors of the torpedoed armed merchant cruiser, HMS *Forfar*. En route to the scene, they carried out a lengthy attack on the Italian submarine *Argo*, which had torpedoed *Saguenay* earlier that day.

On Feburary 23, 1941, *St. Laurent* and *Skeena* sailed from the Firth of Clyde for Halifax, arriving on March 3. Completing refit there, they sailed on July 11 to join the Newfoundland Escort Force, recently formed at St. John's. Thus it was that *St. Laurent* entered upon three years' gruelling duty as a mid-ocean escort, during most of which period she was a member of EG C-1. She was among the earliest Canadian ships to make the "Newfie-Derry" run, arriving at Londonderry in January 1942 from convoy SC.65. She underwent a 3½-month refit at Halifax that year, completing on August 9.

That November *St. Laurent* escorted the collision-damaged *Saguenay* from Cape Race to St. John's, and the following month sailed from the U.K. with convoy ONS.154, which was fated to be roughly handled by the enemy. Late in the evening of December 26 the first victim was torpedoed and sunk. The following day *St. Laurent* and corvettes *Battleford*, *Chilliwack* and *Napanee* teamed up to destroy *U 356*, but 17 other U-boats were in touch with the convoy, and when the action ended on December 30, 14 ships had been sunk.

With the assumption by the RCN of operational control of the West Atlantic in April 1943, the escort groups received the now familiar "C" designations, and *St. Laurent* became a member of C-1. This group, with a U.S. support group including the escort aircraft carrier *Bogue,* was escorting convoy ON.184 in May 1943 when *Bogue*'s aircraft sank *U 569. St. Laurent* picked up 25 survivors. On August 17 she began a long refit at Dartmouth, N.S., working up at Pictou just before the end of the year.

Convoy SC.154, which *St. Laurent* joined on March 2, 1944, was to be a memorable one for her. On the 8th she sent a firefighting party aboard the Swedish M.V. *San Francisco,* whose cargo of flax and pit props was afire, and it was only after seven hours' efforts that the freighter got underway again, with the destroyer's personnel still aboard. *St. Laurent* had no sooner retrieved her firefighters on the 10th when an attack against a U-boat developed. After several hours' attention from *St. Laurent, Owen Sound, Swansea* and HMS *Forester, U 845* surfaced and was disposed of.

In April, *St. Laurent* was allocated to a support group, EG 11, whose particular duty would be to protect Channel shipping during the impending invasion of Normandy. It was an all-River group, the others being *Chaudière, Gatineau, Kootenay,* and *Ottawa* (2nd). After working up at Moville, Ireland, at the end of May, they left for their base at Plymouth. The ensuing six weeks were spent in patrolling the western end of the Channel. *St. Laurent* then being permitted a short rest at 'Derry. She was then assigned a patrol area in the Bay of Biscay where, on August 8, she was near-missed by a glider bomb from a German aircraft. Five days later she picked up the crew of *U 270,* which had sunk following an attack from the air.

▲ *(32) St. Laurent on August 20, 1941, showing early wartime modifications.*

(33) "Sally" taking over the escort of convoy SC.65 at the western rendezvous in January 1942.

(34) *St. Laurent on December 6, 1943, while refitting at Dartmouth, N.S. The two new starboard platforms for 20mm guns are particularly evident.*

(35) *St. Laurent* making smoke during exercises off Larne, Ireland, likely in May 1944 while preparing for her part in D Day operations.

(36) *St. Laurent* in USN-style two-tone paint. "B" gun has been supplanted by a Hedgehog mount, and she has long since acquired her Type 271 RDF lantern and HF/DF mast aft.

In October, a radical change in patrol areas saw *St. Laurent*, *Chaudière* and *Skeena* based on Reykjavik, Iceland. U-boats displaced from their Biscay bases had regrouped in Norway, and the three Rivers had been assigned the task of preventing them from breaking into the Atlantic. On the 24th, severe weather forced the destroyers to seek refuge, and it was at this time that *Skeena* dragged her anchors and was wrecked on Videy Island, near Reykjavik. A party from *St. Laurent* later went aboard her to remove stores and ammunition.

St. Laurent sailed with *Chaudière* and *Qu'Appelle* for Canada as extra escorts to convoy ON.267 in November 1944. On arrival, *St. Laurent* went to Shelburne for refit, following which, on March 20, she and *Restigouche* sailed for Bermuda to work up. Now a member of Halifax Force, she performed local escort duties until VE Day, afterward making several trips as a troop-carrier between Newfoundland and Canada. She also made one round trip in a similar capacity between Canada and Scotland.

On September 24, 1945, with *Ottawa*, *St. Laurent* proceeded to Sydney to de-store, and on October 10 was paid off there. Sold for scrap, she was broken up in 1947 at Lévis by International Iron & Metal Co., Hamilton.

(37) St. Laurent in U.K. waters, c. 1942.

▶ *(38) St. Laurent, 1944-45.*

D/S DATE	GROUP, etc.	STATUS	D/S DATE	GROUP, etc	STATUS	D/S DATE	GROUP, etc.	STATUS
Mar. 2/42	Mid-Ocean Escort	St. John's	Dec. 22/42	MOEF	ON.154	Dec. 7/43	EG C-1, MOEF	Repairs, Dartmouth, N.S.
Mar. 10/42	"	SC.72	Dec. 31/42	"	ON.154	Dec. 21/43	"	Arrived Halifax Dec.17 from Pictou
Mar. 20/42	"	Newport, U.K.	Jan. 8/43	"	Arrived Halifax Dec. 7	Jan. 11/44	"	Arrived Halifax Jan. 9 from A/S sweep
Apr. 2/42	"	ON.81	Jan. 14/43	"	Refitting, Halifax	Jan. 25/44	"	Left Halifax Jan. 24 for St. John's
Apr. 10/42	"	ON.81	Feb. 4/43	"	"	Feb. 8/44	"	U.K.
Apr. 21/42	"	Halifax	Feb. 13/43	"	"	Feb. 22/44	"	Left U.K. Feb. 15 c̄ ON.224
May 1/42	"	Refitting, Halifax	Feb. 23/43	"	En route to St. John's from Halifax	Mar. 7/44	"	Left Argentia Mar. 1 for SC.154
May 11/42	"	"	Mar. 2/43	"	HX.227	Mar. 21/44	"	U.K.
May 21/42	"	"	Mar. 10/43	"	Arrived U.K. Mar. 4	Apr. 11/44	"	Left U.K. Mar. 29 c̄ ONS.32
June 2/42	MOEF	"	Mar. 23/43	"	U.K.	Apr. 25/44	"	Left St. John's Apr. 19 to overtake HXF.287
June 11/42	"	"	Apr. 1/43	EG C-1, MOEF	To overtake ONS.2	May 9/44	11th EG, CiC - WAC	Londonderry
June 22/42	"	"	Apr. 14/43	"	ONS.2	May 23/44	"	"
July 2/42	"	"	Apr. 27/43	"	SC.127	June 6/44	"	Plymouth
July 11/42	"	"	May 3/43	"	Arrived U.K. May 2	June 20/44	11th EG, CiC - Portsmouth	At sea
July 21/42	"	"	May 13/43	"	U.K.	July 4/44	"	At sea
Aug. 1/42	"	"	May 22/43	"	ON.184	July 18/44	11th EG, CiC - Plymouth	Arr. Londonderry July 15
Aug. 11/42	"	En route to St. John's from Halifax	June 2/43	"	Arrived St. John's May 26	Aug. 8/44	"	At sea
Aug. 22/42	"	ON.121	June 12/43	"	HX.242	Aug. 22/44	11th EG, CiC - WAC	Londonderry
Sep. 1/42	"	Arr. St. John's Aug. 29	June 22/43	"	U.K.	Sep. 5/44	"	At sea
Sep. 11/42	"	St. John's	July 6/43	"	Arrived St. John's July 4 from ON.190	Sep. 19/44	"	At sea
Sep. 22/42	"	En route Londonderry from St. John's	July 20/43	"	Left St. John's July 14 to join HX.247	Oct. 3/44	"	Londonderry
Oct. 1/42	"	ON.133	Aug. 3/43	"	Left U.K. Aug. 1 c̄ ON.195	Oct. 24/44	11th EG, CiC - Plymouth	At sea
Oct. 12/42	"	Arr. St. John's Oct. 6	Aug. 17/43	"	Arrived Halifax Aug. 12 from JH.62	Nov. 7/44	11th EG, CiC - WAC	Arrived Londonderry Nov. 5 from Reykjavik
Oct. 22/42	"	At St. John's, making good defects, Oct. 7-22	Sep. 7/43	"	Repairs, Dartmouth	Nov. 21/44	"	En route to ON.267 from A/S search, Nov. 20
Nov. 2/42	"	At St. John's, fitting Type 271 RDF	Sep. 21/43	"	"	Dec. 5/44	11th EG, CiC NWAC	Arrived Halifax Nov. 29 from ON.267
Nov. 11/42	"	ON.143	Oct. 5/43	"	"	Dec. 19/44	"	Repairs, Shelburne
Nov. 20/42	"	Arr. St. John's Nov. 16	Oct. 19/43	"	"	Jan. 9/45	"	"
Dec. 2/42	"	SC.110	Nov. 9/43	"	"	Jan. 23/45	"	"
Dec. 12/42	"	Arr. Londonderry Dec. 4	Nov. 23/43	"	"	Feb. 6/45	"	Arrived Halifax Feb. 2 from Shelburne

See note on p.102

ST. LAURENT

OTTAWA

Launched at Portsmouth on September 30, 1931, HMS *Crusader* spent six years as a member of the 2nd Destroyer Flotilla, Home Fleet, before being sold to the RCN. She was commissioned as HMCS *Ottawa* on June 15, 1938 at Chatham, on the same occasion as HMCS *Restigouche,* and the two left Portland for Canada on September 6.

On October 12, after paying courtesy visits to a number of Quebec and Maritime ports, they left Halifax for Esquimalt. With their arrival there on November 7, the RCN's Western Division could boast a truly homogeneous half-flotilla. In February and March, 1939, the four carried out exercises in the Caribbean with the two destroyers of the Eastern Division and the RN's 8th Cruiser Squadron. Late that May the Western Division escorted the King and Queen from Vancouver to Victoria and back.

The four were again at Vancouver, in connection with the Canadian Pacific Exhibition, on August 31, when it became apparent that war with Germany was imminent. *Fraser* and *St. Laurent* left immediately for Halifax, *Ottawa* and *Restigouche* remaining on the west coast until November 15, when they sailed in their turn. They fuelled from HMAS *Perth* in the Cocos Islands and transited the Panama Canal at the end of the month, arriving at Halifax on December 7.

All four of the erstwhile Western Division ships served as local escort on December 10 to TC.1, the first troop convoy, with the First Canadian Division embarked for Britain. They continued on this duty until late in May 1940, when four of the RCN's six

▲ *(39) HMS Crusader in 1932. She became HMCS Ottawa in 1938.*

▼ *(40) Ottawa on exercises in the Caribbean, 1939. She is apparently acting as flotilla leader.*

destroyers were urgently summoned to the U.K. *Ottawa* could not go, having damaged her stem in collision with the tug *Bansurf* in April. Her repairs completed in mid-June, she returned to her labours as local escort of convoy HX.50.

In mid-August *Ottawa* accompanied convoy TC.7, this time all the way to Britain where, based on the Clyde, she again undertook local escort and rescue duties. On September 22 she joined convoy OB.217 as Senior Officer, and on the 25th had just turned back from it when she was ordered to rejoin. Two ships of the convoy, S.S. *Sulairia* and *Eurymedon*, had been torpedoed. The latter was still afloat, but sinking, and *Ottawa* rescued all survivors except the captain and two officers (who elected to remain aboard), before shaping course to overtake the convoy. On the 26th she was ordered back to the still floating *Eurymedon,* arriving to find her

(41) and (42) Ottawa in two views taken the same date, September 1940. In the view at right it will be noted that her minesweeping davits have been removed. The crane-like fitting overhanging the stern was used in conjunction with winches for streaming paravanes.

(43) and (44) **Ottawa**: *two on-board scenes, likely early in 1940.*

(45) Ottawa, probably early in 1942. The photo combines two negatives.

(46) *Ottawa in 1940. Note the formidable A.A. armament, upper left!*

*(47) **Ottawa**'s ship's company assembled for the traditional group portrait at St. John's, likely in the summer of 1942. Many of these were soon to be numbered among "absent friends". **Skeena** lies alongside.*

▲ *(48) Ottawa on September 18, 1942.*   ▼ *(49) Ottawa in December 1941, wearing typical Western Approaches paint for the period.*

(50) Ottawa at St. John's in 1942, with Saguenay and another, perhaps Skeena.

(51) Ottawa on September 18, 1942. The Type 286M RDF antenna shows to advantage.

surrounded by *Sulairia's* boats. Adding these to those previously rescued, she arrived at Greenock with 118 survivors aboard.

After a brief stay at Glasgow, where she exchanged her after torpedo tubes for a 3-inch anti-aircraft gun, *Ottawa* resumed her duties, principally on WS (U.K. to Middle East) convoys. On November 22 she joined convoy SC.11, rescuing survivors from S.S. *Bussum* the following day. Her occupation remained in general the same into the New Year, and on Feburary 14, 1941, she picked up the crew of the French S.S. *Elisabeth Marie*, bombed and sunk. In June she and her sister Rivers were withdrawn to bolster the recently established Newfoundland Escort Force.

In the next few months *Ottawa* served as mid-ocean escort to two particularly hard-pressed convoys. The first was HX.133, in June, 1941, six of whose 48 ships were sunk. The other was SC.48, in October, which lost nine merchantmen and two of the escort.

On May 29, 1942, *Ottawa* joined SC.85 as Senior Officer of the ocean escort, C-4, having made good several defects that had kept her on local escort work since mid-March. She made four more crossings that summer, and on September 5 left Londonderry to join convoy ON.127 as Senior Officer. The convoy was attacked on the 10th by a large force of U-boats, and near midnight on the 13th *Ottawa* was struck by two torpedoes from *U 91*, the second of which broke her in half. HMS *Celandine* and HMCS *Arvida* together rescued 69 of *Ottawa's* ship's company. Five officers including the C.O., and 109 ratings lost their lives.

D/S DATE	GROUP, etc.	STATUS
Mar. 2/42	Mid-Ocean Escort	CT.11
Mar. 10/42	"	En route to St. John's from Halifax
Mar. 20/42	"	Arrived at Halifax Mar.15
Apr. 2/42	"	En route to Bermuda from Halifax
Apr. 10/42	"	Halifax
Apr. 21/42	"	En route to Halifax from Boston
May 1/42	"	Refitting at Halifax
May 11/42	"	"
May 21/42	"	"
June 2/42	MOEF	SC.85
June 11/42	"	SC.85
June 22/42	"	ON.105
July 2/42	"	Arrived at St. John's 6/30
July 11/42	"	HX.197
July 21/42	"	Arrived Londonderry July 17
Aug. 1/42	"	ON.116
Aug. 11/42	"	Arrived St. John's Aug. 6
Aug. 22/42	"	SC.96
Sep. 1/42	"	Arrived Londonderry Aug.25
Sep. 11/42	"	ON.127
Sep. 22/42		Became war loss, Sept. 14

See note on p.102

OTTAWA

RESTIGOUCHE

HMS *Comet* was launched at Portsmouth on September 30, 1931, the same place and day as her sister, *Crusader*. Both served as members of the 2nd Destroyer Flotilla, Home Fleet, until decommissioned in 1938 for transfer to the RCN. Renamed *Restigouche*, she was commissioned at Chatham on June 15, 1938, still along with *Crusader*, who now became *Ottawa*. The two left Portland for Canada on September 6 and, after paying visits to several eastern Canadian Ports, sailed in mid-October for Esquimalt.

At the end of May, 1939, *Restigouche* and her three sisters of the Western Division escorted the King and Queen from Vancouver to Victoria and back. As earlier recounted, the four were at Vancouver in connection with the Canadian Pacific Exhibition on August 31, when *Fraser* and *St. Laurent* were ordered post-haste to Halifax.

Ottawa and *Restigouche* sailed in their turn for the Atlantic on November 10, refuelling en route from HMAS *Perth* in the Cocos Islands. They passed through the Panama Canal on the 27th, fuelled again at Kingston, Jamaica, and arrived at Halifax on December 7.

The four "C" class sisters sailed on December 10 as local escort to convoy TC.1, carrying 7,400 men of the First Canadian Division to Britain, and a similar function was to be *Restigouche's* lot until the spring of the following year. On May 24, 1940, she, *St. Laurent* and *Skeena* left Halifax for the U.K., the fall of France being imminent. They arrived on May 31 at Plymouth, where their after torpedo tubes were replaced with a more useful 3-inch anti-aircraft gun and their 2-pounder pompoms with quadruple 0.5" machine guns.

On June 9 and 10 *Restigouche* and *St. Laurent*, with several British ships, investigated the French Channel port of Le Havre and St. Valéry-en-Caux, but found no one in urgent need of evacuation. *Restigouche* exchanged a few rounds with a German battery at the latter place. On June 25, with *Fraser*, she went into the Biscay port of St. Jean de Luz, taking off an unusual assortment of civilians and troops, many of them Polish.

As the Canadian destroyers headed for Plymouth, *Fraser* ran afoul of HM cruiser *Calcutta* and was cut in two. *Restigouche* rescued 11 of *Fraser's* officers and 90 ratings, then sent a demolition party aboard to sink her sister's after part, her bow section already having sunk. She arrived the following day at Plymouth, where a part of her ship's company were detailed to assist in taking over a number of French ships lying in the port, as France had capitulated.

Restigouche now assumed patrol, rescue and convoy escort duty out of Plymouth but sailed on July 20 for a new base at Rosyth, Scotland. She put in a few busy weeks as a local escort in that area before sailing for Halifax, where she arrived on September 5 — the first of her class to return from overseas. After two months in refit, *Restigouche* resumed her old role as local escort to eastbound convoys, but only briefly, for her services were again required in the U.K. Assigned to Clyde Escort Force, she arrived overseas late in January 1941, to serve into the spring as escort to convoys entering or leaving British waters.

In May 1941 the Newfoundland

(52) HMS Comet at Valetta, Malta. She became HMCS Restigouche soon afterward.

Escort Force was formed, and on May 30 *Restigouche* and *Ottawa* joined the handful of corvettes that made up that Force. Returning in June from an eastbound convoy, *Restigouche* developed mechanical defects that could be made good only in Halifax, and she arrived there on June 30. Her first post-refit duty entailed taking an M.G.M. film crew to sea to film the crossing of a troop convoy. She left Iceland, westbound, on August 4, and two days later fell in with HMS *Prince of Wales*, carrying Winston Churchill to the Atlantic Conference at Placentia Bay, Newfoundland.

There while fuelling, *Restigouche* touched ground and damaged her screws, requiring repairs at St. John's and then at Halifax. She sailed on October 9, 1941, as escort to convoy TC.14, thus resuming the onerous job of mid-ocean escort. A gale encountered while escorting ON.44 in December caused extensive, though minor damage to deck fittings, and some sprung plates. During refit on the Clyde, which began on Christmas Eve, defects were found in her port turbine, and repairs were not finally completed until March 9, 1942.

Restigouche's first duty on leaving the Clyde was as escort to ON.76, which she escorted all the way to Halifax. She saw one more convoy to the U.K. and another back before docking at Saint John for more repairs, this time to a propeller shaft that had not been right since her grounding at Placentia. She resumed convoy work on September 22 and after two fairly uneventful crossings, set out at the beginning of November with SC.107. This ill-fated convoy lost 15 of its 36 ships.

From then until August 1943, *Restigouche* laboured ceaselessly on the "Newfie-Derry" run, except for one side excursion to Algeria in March with a convoy in support of the North African landings. From early August to mid-December she was refitting on the Tyne, after which she worked up at Tobermory and then resumed her labours with convoy ON.220 in mid-January, 1944. In April she was recalled to the U.K. from a westbound convoy, leaving C-4 to become a member of Escort Group 12 with *Qu'Appelle*, *Saskatchewan* and *Skeena*.

EG 12's duty was to carry out anti-submarine patrols at the west end of the Channel during and after the invasion of Normandy, and on June 7 and 8 did engage in a long, inconclusive action

(53) Libertymen going ashore from **Restigouche** *at Plymouth, June 2, 1940.*

against three U-boats. The destroyers were lucky, as ten acoustic torpedoes were fired at them. At the end of the month the group was allocated to Operation "Dredger", a strike against U-boats and their escorts outbound from Brest. On July 5 they fell upon two inbound U-boats and three armed trawlers, one of which, *V.715*, was sunk. The destroyers received minor damage and some casualties, none fatal.

While her EG 12 consorts were repairing damage, *Restigouche* was assigned temporarily to EG 14, another Canadian support group. While so employed,, she picked up survivors of *U 243*, sunk on July 8 by aircraft. Rejoining EG 12, she shared in a lively action against three armed trawlers south of Brest on August 12. During the action *Qu'Appelle* and *Skeena* collided, and *Restigouche* escorted the latter to Plymouth. She then joined EG 11 with *Chaudière*, *Kootenay* and *Ottawa*, and was with them on patrol when they sank *U 621* on August 18.

Restigouche left Londonderry for

*(54 and 55) Two views of **Restigouche** at Halifax in November 1940. Otherwise unmodified, she has lost her mainmast and after set of torpedo tubes, and acquired a 3" H.A. gun in place of the latter.*

49

home on September 26, in company with *Ottawa,* and in mid-October docked at Saint John for two months' refit. She then took a small convoy to Halifax, where further work was done, but had no sooner commenced working up than she suffered a serious electrical fire. Another month's work was required to make good the damage, and in February 1945 she was allocated to Halifax Force for local escort work.

At the war's end, *Restigouche* made two round trips to the Clyde, bringing home naval personnel and then, on October 6, was paid off at Sydney. She was sold for scrap the following year to International Iron & Metal Co.

*(56) and (57) Two fine views of **Restigouche** on the same occasion, said to be in May 1942. This seems early in view of the fact she already has her HF/DF mast and antenna aft.*

(58) *A beautiful study of* **Restigouche**, *likely early in 1943. She has received her six 20mm guns and Type 271 RDF, and now wears a Type 291 RDF antenna at the masthead. She also appears to be fitted with an unshielded 3" H.A. gun in "X" position.*

D/S DATE	GROUP, etc.	STATUS	D/S DATE	GROUP, etc.	STATUS	D/S DATE	GROUP, etc.	STATUS
Mar. 2/42	Mid-Ocean Escort	Repairs, Greenock	Dec. 22/42	MOEF	SC.112	Dec. 7/43	EG C-4, MOEF	Refitting, Tyne, England.
Mar. 10/42	"	"	Dec. 31/42	"	Arr. Londonderry, Dec. 27	Dec. 21/43	"	Arr. Londonderry, Dec. 18
Mar. 20/42	"	ON.76	Jan. 8/43	"	ON.158	Jan. 11/44	"	Londonderry
Apr. 2/42	"	Halifax	Jan. 14/43	"	ON.158	Jan. 25/44	"	Left U.K. Jan. 16 c̄ ON.220
Apr. 10/42	"	SC.78	Feb. 4/43	"	HX.224	Feb. 8/44	"	Arr. Halifax Feb. 6 from St. John's
Apr. 21/42	"	SC.78	Feb. 13/43	"	Arr. Londonderry, Feb. 4	Feb. 22/44	"	Detached from HX.279 Feb. 21 en route Azores
May 1/42	"	Londonderry	Feb. 23/43	"	Londonderry	Mar. 7/44	"	Left U.K. Feb. 28 c̄ ONS.30
May 11/42	"	Refit, Cardiff	Mar. 2/43	"	Londonderry	Mar. 21/44	"	Left St. John's Mar. 18 for HX.283
May 21/42	"	"	Mar. 10/43	"	Londonderry	Apr. 11/44	"	Arr. Liverpool Apr. 8 from Belfast
June 2/42	MOEF	"	Mar. 23/43	"	Left Algiers Mar. 10	Apr. 25/44	"	Liverpool
June 11/42	"	"	Apr. 1/43	EG C-4, MOEF	Arr. U.K. Mar. 25	May 9/44	12th EG, CiC - WAC	Londonderry
June 22/42	"	Arr. St. John's, June 21	Apr. 14/43	"	ON.177	May 23/44	12th EG, RCN	Left L'pool May 21 for Clyde
July 2/42	"	Arr. Halifax for repairs, June 30	Apr. 27/43	"	HX 235	June 6/44	"	Plymouth
July 11/42	"	Arr. Saint John, N.B. for repairs, July 3	May 3/43	"	Arr. Londonderry, May 2	June 20/44	"	At sea
July 21/42	"	Saint John	May 13/43	"	Londonderry	July 4/44	"	At sea
Aug. 1/42	"	"	May 22/43	"	ONS.8	July 18/44	"	At sea
Aug. 11/42	"	"	June 2/43	"	Arr. St. John's, May 28	Aug. 8/44	"	Londonderry
Aug. 22/42	"	"	June 12/43	"	SC.133	Aug. 22/44	12th EG, CiC - WAC	Liverpool
Sep. 1/42	"	"	June 22/43	EG C-3, MOEF	U.K. Port	Sep. 5/44	"	Repairs, Liverpool
Sep. 11/42	"	"	July 6/43	"	Left U.K. July 4 c̄ ONS.12	Sept. 19/44	11th EG, CiC - WAC	At sea
Sep. 22/42	"	Arr. St. John's, Sept. 21	July 20/43	EG C-4, MOEF	Arr. St. John's, July 17	Oct. 3/44	"	Left St. John's Oct. 2 for Halifax
Oct. 1/42	"	SC.101	Aug. 3/43	"	Arr. U.K. from SC.137	Oct. 24/44	11th EG, CiC Plym.	Refitting Saint John, N.B.
Oct. 12/42	"	Arr. Londonderry, Oct. 11	Aug. 17/43	"	Refitting, Jarrow	Nov. 7/44	11th EG, CiC - WAC	"
Oct. 22/42	"	ON.137	Sep. 7/43	"	Refitting, Tyne	Nov. 21/44	"	"
Nov. 2/42	"	SC.107	Sep. 21/42	"	"	Dec. 5/44	11th EG, CiC NWAC	"
Nov. 11/42	"	Arr. Londonderry, Nov. 10	Oct. 5/43	"	"	Dec. 19/44	"	Refit completed Dec. 14
Nov. 20/42	"	ON.147	Oct. 19/43	"	"	Jan. 9/45	"	Repairing, Halifax
Dec. 2/42	"	Arr. Halifax, Nov. 30	Nov. 9/43	"	"	Jan. 23/45	"	"
Dec. 12/42	"	SC.112	Nov. 23/43	"	"	Feb. 6/45	"	Left Halifax Feb. 4 for Bermuda

See note on p.102

RESTIGOUCHE

ASSINIBOINE

The transfer of HMS *Kempenfelt* to the RCN completed our acquisition of the "C" class half-flotilla, she having been its leader. She was launched at Cowes, Isle of Wight, in October 1930, and on commissioning became a member of the 2nd Destroyer Flotilla, Home Fleet. At the end of 1938 she joined the Plymouth Local Defence Flotilla, transferring to the 18th Destroyer Flotilla, Channel Force, on the outbreak of the war.

She was commissioned HMCS *Assiniboine* at Devonport on October 19, 1939, and on November 9 sailed for Halifax. She arrived there on the 17th

*(59) HMS **Kempenfelt** on exercises in 1934. She was to become HMCS **Assiniboine** five years later.*

(60) and (61) Two views of Assiniboine at Halifax in December 1940.

and was on escort duty the following day with convoy HX.9. Three days later, with *St. Laurent*, she returned to Halifax escorting HMS *Emerald,* the latter laden with gold bullion from the Bank of England.

On December 8, *Assiniboine* arrived at Kingston, Jamaica, to relieve a probably ungrateful *Restigouche* on that station. Her duty would be to intercept German merchant ships attempting to escape home from those waters. The patrols were uneventful until March 6, 1940, when the German M.V. *Hannover* was caught by HMS *Dunedin* and set afire by her own crew. Called to the scene by *Dunedin*, *Assiniboine* took the freighter in tow while the cruiser fought the fires. The two warships later exchanged roles, arriving with their smouldering prize at Kingston on March 13. Rebuilt, *Hannover* became the first of the escort aircraft carriers, HMS *Audacity*.

Assiniboine was now called home, arriving at Halifax on March 31. Toward the end of May she was docked at Saint John for a short refit, after which she resumed service as a local escort. On January 15, 1941, with *Restigouche* and two of the RCN's lately acquired, ex-American destroyers — *Columbia* and *St. Francis* — she sailed for the U.K. to join EG 10 at Greenock. On February 28 she rescued survivors of S.S. *Anchises,* sunk by aircraft west of Ireland.

Assiniboine was damaged on April 5 in the Irish Sea, when she collided with M.V. *Lairdswood,* and emerged from the dockyard at Greenock on May 22,

in time to play an offstage role in the *Bismarck* pursuit as escort to HMS *Repulse*. She refuelled at Hvalfjord, Iceland, on May 25, but the action was by then beyond her range and she was ordered to Greenock about the time *Bismarck* was finally sunk on May 27.

The Newfoundland Escort Force having been formed at the end of May, *Assiniboine* was now recalled to augment it. Her most memorable duty as a member of this force came early in August when, with *Restigouche*, she helped screen HMS *Prince of Wales* from mid-Atlantic to Placentia Bay, Newfoundland. The battleship was carrying Winston Churchill to the historic Atlantic Charter meeting with President Roosevelt. *Assiniboine* and *Saguenay* were among Churchill's escort as far as Iceland on his way home, and on August 16, *Assiniboine* ferried him from the battleship to the jetty at Reykjavik and back. She then returned to her duties as mid-ocean escort with EG 14.

On August 2, 1942, she was part of the escort of convoy SC.94, which was sighted and immediately attacked by a member of a wolf pack. Late the following afternoon *Assiniboine* surprised *U 210* on the surface, and a gun action followed at close range. *Assiniboine* finally succeeded in ramming her adversary and the U-boat was scuttled, 38 survivors being rescued. The destroyer suffered one fatal casualty, O/Smn Kenneth Watson, RCN, and a dozen wounded. With her stem bent and much damage to her bridge and forward gunshields, she arrived back at St. John's on August 9. A couple of weeks later she arrived at Halifax for a long refit. On February 26, 1943, she sailed for Londonderry to

(62) *Assiniboine leaving Halifax on September 30, 1940, to join convoy HX.77 as local escort, Saguenay following.*

▲ (63) *Assiniboine on March 19, 1942. Note splinter mats around her wheelhouse.*

▼ (64) *Assiniboine: a view for'ard from "X" gundeck, showing the 3" gun that replaced her after torpedo tubes in 1940.*

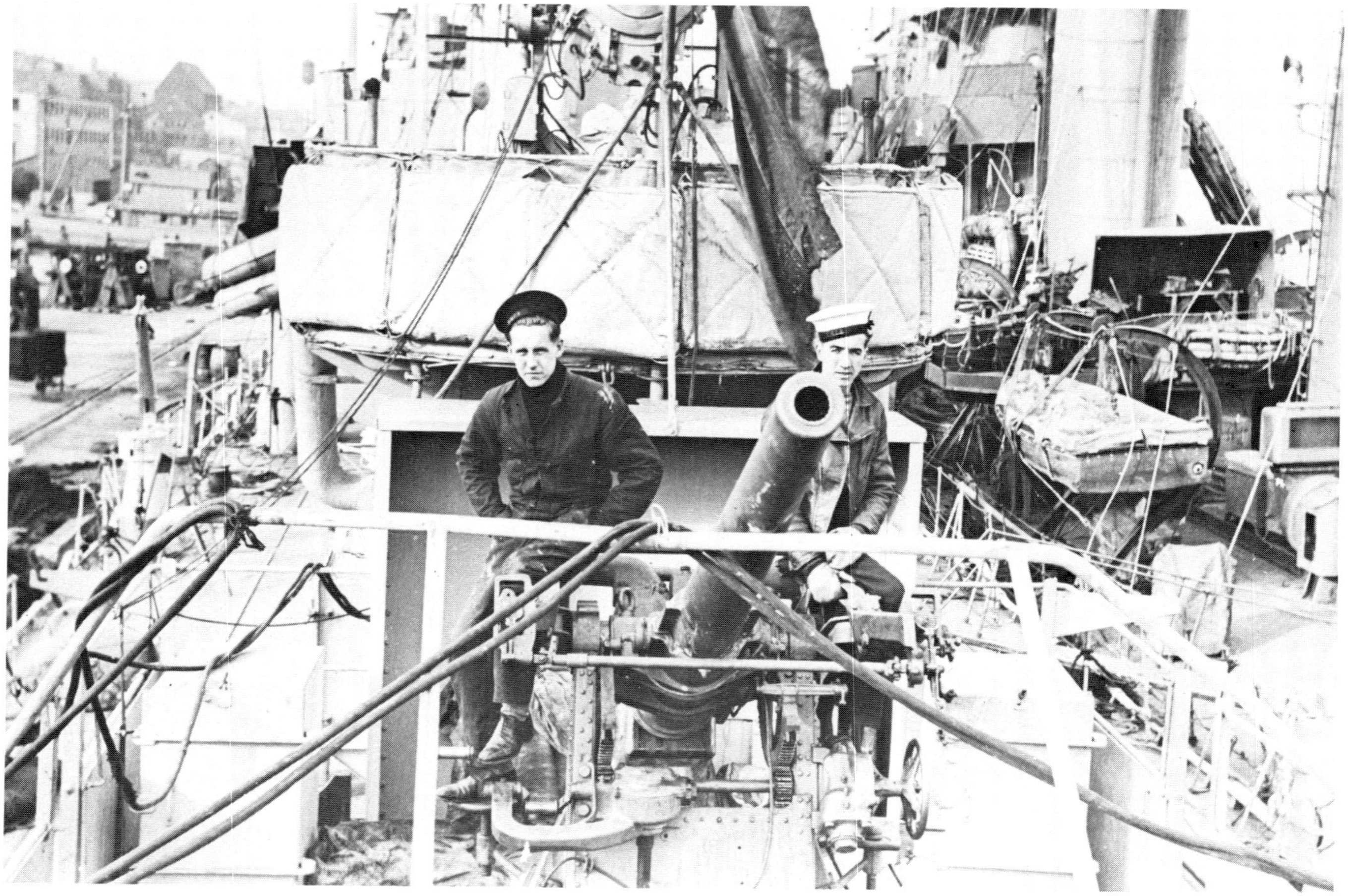

(65) to (67) Above and right: *Assiniboine* at St. John's on August 9, 1942, three days after ramming and sinking U 210. Note her bent forefoot. Below: under repairs at Halifax, September 16.

join EG C-3, en route tangling once more (March 2) with a surfaced U-boat. Both were severely damaged in the encounter, and *Assiniboine* spent 4½ months under repair at Liverpool.

Back in service, she joined EG C-1, and by the spring of 1944 had escorted 13 convoys on the "Newfie-Derry" run. On April 20 she went into refit at Shelburne, N.S., following which she was allocated to EG 12. She arrived at 'Derry on August 1, carried out exercises and by August 9 was on patrol at the west end of the Channel. On the night of August 11-12, with *Qu'Appelle, Restigouche, Skeena* and HMS *Albrighton,* she took part in an action against three armed trawlers in Audierne Bay.

Assiniboine now transferred, first to EG 14 — with which on August 25 she screened HMS *Warspite,* who was shelling Brest — then to EG 11 early in September. On September 1 she was detached to assist EG 9 in attacking and destroying *U 247* near Wolf Rock.

In October, EG 11 resumed patrol duty in the Iceland area, with a view to intercepting Norway-based U-boats en route to the Atlantic. It was while sheltering from a gale there that one of the group, *Skeena,* was lost by stranding. *Assiniboine* rejoined EG 14 at the beginning of 1945, and on February 14 collided with S.S. *Empire Bond* in the Channel. Repairs at Sheerness were not completed until early in March, after which the ship was employed at a variety of tasks until the end of the European war. She then embarked Canadian servicemen at

(68) Assiniboine at high speed, probably in 1941 — a good portrait, incidentally, of a quadruple .5" machine gun.

(69) As apt a study as one could wish of a destroyer at work: **Assiniboine** *at sea with a convoy in 1943. Her 3" H.A. gun has been re-sited in "X" position.*

(70) Assiniboine, likely in 1942 before her scrap with U 210.

Greenock, reaching Halifax on June 6, and made another trip as a makeshift troopship from St. John's to Quebec City before suffering a boiler room fire off the Saguenay River on July 4.

Not deemed worth repairing, she was towed to Sorel and paid off there on August 8. On November 7 she broke away from the former HMCS *West York,* which was towing her to Baltimore to be broken up, and went aground on the eastern tip of Prince Edward Island. Her skeleton still lies there.

(71) and (72) Below left, Assiniboine at Sorel in 1945, awaiting sale for scrap along with a group of corvettes. At right, her wartime nickname, "Bones", all too prophetic, she lies on Prince Edward Island in 1961.

D/S DATE	GROUP, etc.	STATUS	D/S DATE	GROUP, etc.	STATUS	D/S DATE	GROUP, etc.	STATUS
Mar. 2/42	Mid-Ocean Escort	Londonderry	Dec. 22/42	MOEF	Refitting, Halifax	Dec. 7/43	EG C-1, MOEF	Left U.K. Nov. 27 c̄ ON.213
Mar. 10/42	"	"	Dec. 31/42	"	En route to St. John's	Dec. 21/43	"	Left St. John's Dec. 14 for HX.270
Mar. 20/42	"	ON.74	Jan. 8/43	"	HX.221	Jan. 11/44	"	Left U.K. Jan. 9 c̄ ON.219
Apr. 2/42	"	St. John's	Jan. 14/43	"	Arr. Londonderry Jan. 13	Jan. 25/44	"	Arr. St. John's Jan. 21 from ON.219
Apr. 10/42	"	SC.77	Feb. 4/43	"	ON.163	Feb. 8/44	" (S.O.)	U.K.
Apr. 21/42	"	Londonderry	Feb. 13/43	"	Arr. Halifax Feb.12 for repairs	Feb. 22/44	" (S.O.)	Left U.K. Feb. 15 c̄ ON.224
May 1/42	"	ON.88	Feb. 23/43	"	Repairs completed Feb. 20 To sail for Londonderry	Mar. 7/44	" (S.O.)	Left Argentia March 2 to overtake SC.154
May 11/42	"	St. John's	Mar. 2/43	"	En route Londonderry from Halifax	Mar. 21/44	" (S.O.)	U.K.
May 21/42	"	Londonderry	Mar. 10/43	"	Arrived in U.K. Mar. 7; To refit at Liverpool	Apr. 11/44	" (S.O.)	Left U.K. Mar. 29 c̄ ONS.32
June 2/42	MOEF	"	Mar. 23/43	"	Repairs, Liverpool	Apr. 25/44	" (S.O.)	Refitting, Halifax
June 11/42	"	ON.100	Apr. 1/43	"	"	May 9/44	12th EG, CiC - WAC	Refitting, Shelburne
June 22/42	"	Arrived St. John's 6/14	Apr. 14/43	"	"	May 23/44	12th EG, RCN	"
July 2/42	"	HX.195	Apr. 27/43	"	"	June 6/44	"	"
July 11/42	"	Arr. Londonderry July 3	May 3/43	"	"	June 20/44	"	"
July 21/42	"	ON.112	May 13/43	"	"	July 4/44	"	Left Shelburne June 29 for Halifax
Aug. 1/42	"	Arr. St. John's July 26	May 22/43	EG C-3, MOEF	"	July 18/44	"	Bermuda
Aug. 11/42	"	Arr. St. John's Aug. 9	June 2/43	"	"	Aug. 8/44	"	Arr. Londonderry Aug. 1 from St. John's
Aug. 22/42	"	Repairing, St. John's	June 12/43	EG C-1, MOEF	"	Aug. 22/44	12th EG, CiC - WAC	At sea
Sep. 1/42	"	Arr. Halifax Aug. 24	June 22/43	"	"	Sep. 5/44	"	Arr. Liverpool Aug. 29 from Plymouth
Sep. 11/42	"	Refitting, Halifax	July 6/43	"	"	Sep. 19/44	11th EG, CiC - WAC	At sea
Sep. 22/42	"	"	July 20/43	"	At Liverpool; Repairs completed July 13	Oct. 3/44	"	At sea
Oct. 1/42	"	"	Aug. 3/43	"	Left U.K. Aug. 1 c̄ ON.195	Oct. 24/44	11th EG CiC - Plymouth	At sea
Oct. 12/42	"	"	Aug. 17/43	"	St. John's	Nov. 7/44	11th EG, CiC - WAC	Arr. Londonderry Nov. 5 from Reykjavik
Oct. 22/42	"	"	Sep. 7/43	"	U.K.	Nov. 21/44	"	At sea
Nov. 2/42	"	"	Sep. 21/43	"	En route Halifax Sept. 18 from ON.201	Dec. 5/44	11th EG, CiC - NWAC	Milford Haven
Nov. 11/42	"	"	Oct. 5/43	"	Left St. John's Sep.27 for HX.258	Dec. 19/44	"	Liverpool, U.K.
Nov. 20/42	"	"	Oct. 19/43	"	U.K.	Jan. 9/45	"	At sea
Dec. 2/42	"	"	Nov. 9/43	"	Left St. John's Nov. 4 for HX.264	Jan. 23/45	"	At sea
Dec. 12/42	"	"	Nov. 23/43	"	U.K.	Feb. 6/45	"	Arr. Belfast Feb. 2 from Liverpool

See note on p.102

ASSINIBOINE

MARGAREE

Negotiations begun in July 1940 for a destroyer to replace the lost *Fraser* resulted in the purchase of HMS *Diana*. She had been launched on the Tyne in June 1932, and commissioned that December for service with the 1st Destroyer Flotilla, Mediterranean. A year later she was transferred to the 8th Flotilla, China Station but was again in the Mediterranean between September 1935 and July 1936. She had returned to the China Station before the outbreak of the war, attached to the 21st Flotilla, but found herself yet again in the Mediterranean when the whole flotilla was transferred there in 1939. *Diana* returned to home waters that December, and in 1940 saw service in the Norwegian campaign as a member of the 3rd Destroyer Flotilla, Home Fleet.

Diana was transferred to the RCN as *Margaree* at Londonderry on September 6, 1940. She was commissioned before refitting, and this work was carried out in London's Albert Docks at the height of the blitz. The ship arrived at Londonderry on October 20, and immediately sailed to pick up OL.8, a five-ship convoy whose sole escort she would be.

Two days later, some 400 miles west of Ireland, *Margaree* crossed the bows of one of her charges, M.V. *Port Fairy,* and was cut in half just abaft the bridge. The forward half sank immediately, taking everyone aboard down with it, but six officers and 28 men were rescued by *Port Fairy* from the after section. As it appeared that this portion might remain afloat indefinitely, *Port Fairy* attempted to sink it with gunfire, but ran out of ammunition and finally left the wreck burning and very low in the water.

Four officers, including the C.O., and 138 men were lost in *Margaree*, and ironically most of them were survivors of *Fraser's* sinking four months earlier, in almost identical fashion.

(73) HMS *Diana* in 1933. She was to become HMCS *Margaree* briefly in 1940.

(74) Seemingly the only surviving photo of *Margaree* during her short career as a Canadian ship, this was taken from the freighter *Port Fairy*, which had accidentally cut her in half. It was published three weeks later in the *Toronto Star*.

OTTAWA (2nd)

Originally HMS *Griffin*, she was launched at Barrow-in-Furness in August 1935, and joined the 20th Destroyer Flotilla in the Mediterranean the following spring. The flotilla was soon afterward redesignated the 1st Destroyer Flotilla, and at the end of 1939 shifted its base to Harwich, England. *Griffin* took part in the evacuation of Namsos, Norway, in May 1940, and that October, with *Gallant* and *Hotspur,* sank the Italian submarine *Lafole* near Gibraltar.

In 1941 *Griffin* rejoined the Mediterranean Fleet, and during the ensuing 18 months was in the thick of the action in that theatre of war. In particular, she was present at the battle of Cape Matapan in March 1941, and did yeoman service during the evacuation of Crete the following month.

She returned to the U.K. at the beginning of 1943 to refit, following which she was transferred to the RCN as a replacement for the lost *Ottawa*. She was commissioned at Southampton on March 20, still bearing her original name, and her commanding officer, Cdr. H.F. Pullen, would have preferred to leave matters so. However, on April 10 she was renamed *Ottawa* in conformity with the "river" nomenclature of her class.

The new *Ottawa* worked up at Tobermory, April 21-30, then joined convoy ON.182 as Senior Officer of

▲ (75) HMS *Griffin*, who became HMCS *Ottawa* (2nd) in 1943.

(76) *Ottawa* on November 22, 1943, with convoy ON.211.

*(77) **Ottawa** on October 9, 1943, while refitting at Halifax.*

EG C-5. After several uneventful Atlantic crossings, she was allocated to the EG 11 as S.O., the other members being *Chaudière, Gatineau, Kootenay* and *St. Laurent*. The group's Channel patrol, begun on June 5, 1944, proceeded without incident until July 6, when *Ottawa* and *Kootenay* were detached to assist HMS *Statice* with a contact off Beachy Head. The three belaboured the target for some 13 hours before it was concluded, rightly, that the U-boat had been destroyed. It later proved to have been *U 678*.

On August 18, *Ottawa, Kootenay,* and *Chaudière* carried out an attack of comparable duration off LaRochelle, in the Bay of Biscay, thus disposing of *U 621,* and two days later the same trio sank *U 984* west of Brest.

On September 25, *Ottawa* and *Restigouche* left Londonderry for Canada, and on October 12 *Ottawa* commenced a long refit at Saint John. She returned to service on February 26, 1945, but remained in Canadian waters. On March 11, while carrying out an anti-submarine sweep off Halifax, she was involved in collision with HMCS *Stratford,* both receiving considerable damage to their bows.

Repairs were completed at the end of April, and on May 8 the European war came to an end. *Ottawa* was now put to use as a troop carrier, making several trips between St. John's and Halifax or Quebec City, and four to Greenock, Scotland, in this role. On November 1, 1945, she was paid off at Sydney and, in August 1946, sold for scrap to International Iron & Metal Co.

*(78) Another view of **Ottawa** on October 9, 1943. Note the "griffin" badge on the funnel, surmounted by the "barber pole" insignia of C.5 Escort Group.*

(79) and (80) **Ottawa** *in May 1943 (above) and in the Bay of Biscay on August 20, 1944.*

D/S DATE	GROUP, etc.	STATUS	D/S DATE	GROUP, etc.	STATUS
			Dec. 7/43	EG C-5, MOEF	Refitting, Halifax
			Dec. 21/43	"	"
			Jan. 11/44	"	Left St. John's Jan. 10 for HX.274
			Jan. 25/44	"	U.K.
			Feb. 8/44	"	Left U.K. Jan. 31 c̄ ON.222
			Feb. 22/44	" (S.O.)	Left St. John's Feb. 18 for SC.153
			Mar. 7/44	" (S.O.)	U.K.
			Mar. 21/44	" (S.O.)	Left U.K. Mar. 14 c̄ ONS.31
			Apr. 11/44	" (S.O.)	Left St. John's April 1 for HX.285
Mar. 23/43	–	Commissioned in U.K., 3/20	Apr. 25/44	" (S.O.)	U.K.
Apr. 1/43	–	Southampton	May 9/44	11th EG, CiC – WAC	Londonderry
Apr. 14/43	–	To be ready for sea, May 3	May 23/44	"	"
Apr. 27/43	–	Arr. Tobermory Apr. 20	June 6/44	" (S.O.)	Plymouth
May 3/43	–	Tobermory	June 20/44	" (S.O.) CiC – Portsmouth	At sea
May 13/43	EG C-5, MOEF	ON.182	July 4/44	" (S.O.)	At sea
May 22/43	"	Arr. St. John's May 17	July 18/44	11th EG (S.O.) CiC – Plymouth	Arr. Londonderry July 15 from patrol
June 2/43	"	HX.240	Aug. 8/44	" (S.O.)	At sea
June 12/43	"	ON.188	Aug. 22/44	11th EG, CiC – WAC (S.O.)	Londonderry
June 22/43	"	Arr. St. John's June 20	Sep. 5/44	" (S.O.)	At sea
July 6/43	"	Arr. U.K. from HX.245	Sep. 19/44	" (S.O.)	At sea
July 20/43	"	Left U.K. July 18 c̄ ON.193	Oct. 3/44	" (S.O.)	Left St. John's Oct. 2 for Halifax
Aug. 3/43	"	Arr. St. John's July 25 from ON.193	Oct. 24/44	11th EG (S.O.) CiC – Plymouth	Refitting, Saint John
Aug. 17/43	"	Arr. U.K. Aug. 12 from HX.250	Nov. 7/44	11th EG, CiC – WAC	"
Sep. 7/43	"	Arr. St. John's Sept. 4 from ON.199	Nov. 21/44	"	"
Sep. 21/43	"	Arr. Halifax Sept. 19 from St. John's	Dec. 5/44	11th EG, CiC – NWAC	"
Oct. 5/43	"	Refitting, Halifax	Dec. 19/44	"	"
Oct. 19/43	"	"	Jan. 9/45	"	"
Nov. 9/43	"	U.K.	Jan. 23/45	"	"
Nov. 23/43	"	Left U.K. Nov. 21 c̄ ON.211	Feb. 6/45	"	"

See note on p.102

OTTAWA (2nd)

KOOTENAY

As HMS *Decoy,* she was launched in June 1932 at Southampton and commissioned the following spring with the 1st Destroyer Flotilla, Mediterranean Fleet. In December 1934 she relieved HMS *Witch* on the China Station, transferring to the 8th Flotilla, but in 1935 was detached for service in the Red Sea and Mediterranean.

Decoy returned to the China Station in 1936, remaining there until the fall of 1939, when she transferred to the 21st Flotilla and shortly found herself yet again in the Mediterranean. Almost continuously in action, and seemingly bearing a charmed life, she took part in the evacuation of Greece and Crete and escorted Tobruk convoys, as well as screening large fleet units in a variety of coastal operations.

She spent six months with the Eastern Fleet in the Pacific after the attack on Pearl Harbor, then returned to Britain for a badly needed refit at Jarrow-on-Tyne. On completion of this, *Decoy* was commissioned there on April 12, 1943, as HMCS *Kootenay*. At the end of May she joined Escort Group C-5, the "Barber Pole Brigade", and for the succeeding year trudged to and fro on the "Newfie-Derry" run. She found this task fairly uneventful, not to say dull, as the U-boats had suffered a major defeat at the beginning of May and had largely been withdrawn.

On April 25, 1944, *Kootenay* was transferred to EG 11 with *Chaudière, Gatineau, Ottawa* and *St. Laurent.* The

(81) HMS **Decoy**, who became HMCS **Kootenay** in 1943.

▶ (82) *Kootenay* arriving in Halifax in February 1944 from convoy ON.222.

(83) *Kootenay* in Halifax in February 1944.

(84) Kootenay in Halifax in February 1944.

(85) Kootenay docking for repairs in Halifax, presumably in November 1943.

group was intended to counter the expected U-boat onslaught against Channel traffic during and after the impending invasion of France.

Their patrol began on D Day, June 6, but a month was to pass before *Kootenay* tasted blood. On July 6 she and *Ottawa* went to assist HMS *Statice*, who had a promising asdic contact southwest of Beachy Head. The three carried out a prolonged attack on the target, finally destroying *U 678*. On August 18, with *Ottawa* and *Chaudière*, *Kootenay* sank *U 621* off the mouth of the Gironde River, and two days later the same team destroyed *U 984* off Brest.

EG 11 now proceeded to Londonderry, leaving *Kootenay* at Plymouth with a defective feed pump. This was repaired at Devonport, but the

(86) Kootenay at rest in a U.K. anchorage.

(87) Kootenay off Quebec City in the summer of 1945.

ship needed other ills attended to, and so sailed for home from Plymouth, escorting convoy ONS.254.

She emerged from refit at Shelburne at the end of February 1945, crossed to 'Derry with HX.345 and worked up at Tobermory in April. Back with EG 11, she was at sea on a last, short patrol when the European war ended, and she sailed once more for home at the end of May, carrying a number of Canadian servicemen embarked at Greenock. She continued "trooping" between St. John's and Quebec City for three months, making six round trips, and on October 26 was paid off at Sydney. Sold in 1946, she was broken up at Lévis by International Iron & Metal Co., Hamilton.

*(88) A view aft to port, showing two of **Kootenay**'s six Oerlikons.*

*(89) **Kootenay** making smoke as she retires under fire of a German battery on the Biscay coast, August 24, 1944.*

			D/S DATE	GROUP, etc.	STATUS	D/S DATE	GROUP, etc.	STATUS
						Dec. 7/43	EG C-5, MOEF	Left St. John's Dec. 1 for HX.268
						Dec. 21/43	"	U.K.
						Jan. 11/44	"	Left St. John's Jan. 10 for HX.274
						Jan. 25/44	"	U.K.
						Feb. 8/44	"	Left U.K. Jan. 31 c̄ ON.222
						Feb. 22/44	"	Left Halifax Feb. 19 to overtake SC.153
						Mar. 7/44	"	U.K.
						Mar. 21/44	"	Left U.K. Mar. 14 c̄ ONS.31
						Apr. 11/44	"	Left St. John's Apr. 1 for HX.285
						Apr. 25/44	"	U.K.
						May 9/44	11th EG, CiC - WAC	Londonderry
			Apr. 14/43	-	Commissioned in U.K. Apr.12	May 23/44	"	"
			Apr. 27/43	-	U.K.	June 6/44	"	Plymouth
			May 3/43	-	"	June 20/44	11th EG, CiC - Portsmouth	At sea
			May 13/43	-	"	July 4/44	"	At sea
			May 22/43	-	"	July 18/44	11th EG, CiC - Plymouth	Arr. Londonderry July 15 from patrol
			June 2/43	EG C-5, MOEF	HX.240	Aug. 8/44	"	At sea
			June 12/43	"	ON.188	Aug. 22/44	11th EG, CiC - WAC	Londonderry
			June 22/43	"	En route St. John's	Sep. 5/44	"	At sea
			July 6/43	"	Arr. U.K. from HX.245	Sep. 19/44	"	Left U.K. Sept. 17 c̄ ONS.254
			July 20/43	"	Left U.K. July 18 c̄ ON.193	Oct. 3/44	"	Arrived Shelburne Oct. 1 from Halifax
			Aug. 3/43	"	Arr. St. John's July 25 from ON.193	Oct. 24/44	11th EG, CiC - Plymouth	Refitting, Shelburne
			Aug. 17/43	"	Arrived U.K. Aug. 12 from HX.250	Nov. 7/44	11th RG, CiC - WAC	"
			Sep. 7/43	"	Arr. Halifax Sept. 5 from ON.199	Nov. 21/44	"	"
			Sep. 21/43	"	Left St. John's Sept. 14 for HX.256	Dec. 5/44	11th EG, CiC - NWAC	"
			Oct. 5/43	"	U.K.	Dec. 19/44	"	"
			Oct. 19/43	"	Arr. St. John's Oct. 18 from ON.205	Jan. 9/45	"	"
			Nov. 9/43	"	Repairs, Halifax	Jan. 23/45	"	"
			Nov. 23/43	"	"	Feb. 6/45	"	"

See note on p.102

KOOTENAY

SASKATCHEWAN

As HMS *Fortune,* she was launched on the Clyde in August 1934 and commissioned on May 8, 1935 for service with the 6th Destroyer Flotilla, Home Fleet. Between then and the fall of 1939 she spent a good deal of her time in the Mediterranean and the Bay of Biscay, on patrol duties occasioned by the Spanish civil war.

Fortune was at Scapa Flow with the 8th Flotilla, however, when World War 2 broke out, and 17 days later, on September 20, shared with *Forester* in the destruction of *U 27* west of the Hebrides. On March 20, 1940, while screening larger fleet units north of the Shetlands, *Fortune* joined *Faulknor* and *Firedrake* in sinking *U 44.* During the following month she took part in operations off Norway.

In September 1940 *Fortune* was present at the "melancholy action" against the Vichy-controlled French fleet at Oran, and soon afterward entered upon a period of service in the Mediterranean. There, in May 1941, she was damaged by a near-miss bomb while escorting a Malta convoy, and spent six months under repair at Chatham.

Fortune spent part of the following 18 months in the Indian Ocean and part in the south Atlantic before undergoing a refit at London. At the conclusion of this she was transferred to the RCN and commissioned as *Saskatchewan* on May 31, 1943. Assigned to Escort Group C-3 as Senior Officer, she spent the succeeding year on the north Atlantic. The only noteworthy event during this period seems to have been a minor sideswipe with the U.S. destroyer *Kendrick* in the River Foyle, in January 1944.

(90) HMS Fortune in May 1943, shortly before becoming Saskatchewan.

▼ *(91) Saskatchewan on December 8, 1944.*

In May 1944 *Saskatchewan* transferred to EG 12, with which she was to patrol the Channel and its approaches during and after D Day. The highlight of this period was Operation "Dredger", in which, with *Qu'Appelle* and *Skeena*, she sank one armed trawler and severely damaged two others. During the action, which took place off Brest during the night of July 5/6, *Saskatchewan* sustained five casualties, one of them fatal.

EG 12 returned to 'Derry at the end of July, and *Saskatchewan* then sailed independently for home. She arrived on August 6 at Halifax, and later that month went into refit at Shelburne. This was completed early in November, but further work soon proved necessary, and this was undertaken at St. John's.

Saskatchewan returned to the U.K. in mid-January 1945, and for the next few months served first with EG 14 and then with EG 11. She was at Plymouth on VE Day, and on May 30 left Greenock for Halifax, carrying a number of returning Canadian personnel. Like others of her class, she was now put to use carrying other personnel from St. John's to Quebec City, and she made five such trips before being declared surplus on September 23. She was finally paid off at Sydney on January 28, 1946, and sold later that year to International Iron & Metal Co., Hamilton, for scrap.

(92) Saskatchewan, August 13, 1943, with convoy HX.249.

(93) Saskatchewan at "Newfiejohn" in July 1942. Note the shrouded Hedgehog mounts abreast "A" gun. The ship alongside is HMS Burnham.

▲ *(94) Saskatchewan, probably in 1943.*

▼ *(95) Saskatchewan in 1944. Note the bow chaser!*

(96) *Saskatchewan on December 8, 1944, at Halifax.*

(97) *Saskatchewan* at sea on January 12, 1945, following repairs at St. John's.

(98) *Saskatchewan* arriving at Sydney on October 1, 1945, to pay off for disposal.

(99) Saskatchewan leaving St. John's on one of her personnel-carrying trips during the summer of 1945.

D/S DATE	GROUP, etc.	STATUS	D/S DATE	GROUP, etc.	STATUS
			Dec. 7/43	EG C-3, MOEF	U.K.
			Dec. 21/43	"	Left U.K. Dec. 17 for ON.216
			Jan. 11/44	"	Left St. John's Jan. 3 for SC.150
			Jan. 25/44	"	U.K.
			Feb. 8/44	"	Left U.K. Jan. 29 c ONS.28
			Feb. 22/44	"	Left St. John's Feb. 17 for HX.279
			Mar. 7/44	"	U.K.
			Mar. 21/44	"	Arr. St. John's Mar. 18 from ON.227
			Apr. 11/44	"	Londonderry
			Apr. 25/44	"	"
			May 9/44	12th EG, CiC – WAC	"
			May 23/44	12th EG, RCN	"
			June 6/44	"	Plymouth
			June 20/44	"	At sea
			July 4/44	"	At sea
			July 18/44	"	At sea
June 2/43	–	Commissioned in U.K., 5/31	Aug. 8/44	"	Arr. Halifax Aug. 6 from St. John's
June 12/43	–	U.K.	Aug. 22/44	12th EG, CiC – WAC	Refitting, Shelburne
June 22/43	EG C-3, MOEF	U.K.	Sep. 5/44	"	"
July 6/43	"	U.K.	Sep. 19/44	11th EG, CiC – WAC	"
July 20/43	"	Arr. St. John's July 18 from ON.192	Oct. 3/44	"	"
Aug. 3/43	"	Left St. John's July 28 for HX.249	Oct. 24/44	11th EG, CiC – Plymouth	"
Aug. 17/43	"	U.K.	Nov. 7/44	11th EG, CiC – WAC	"
Sep. 7/43	"	Arr. St. John's Sept. 5 from Halifax	Nov. 21/44	"	Halifax
Sep. 21/43	"	U.K.	Dec. 5/44	11th EG, CiC – NWAC	"
Oct. 5/43	"	Left U.K. Sep. 27 c ONS.19	Dec. 19/44	"	St. John's
Oct. 19/43	"	Left St. John's Oct. 16 for HX.261	Jan. 9/45	"	Repairs, St. John's
Nov. 9/43	"	U.K.	Jan. 23/45	"	Left Londonderry Jan. 21 for Tobermory
Nov. 23/43	"	Left St. John's Nov. 22 for SC.147	Feb. 6/45	"	Tobermory, WUP

See note on p.102

SASKATCHEWAN

GATINEAU

Originally HMS *Express,* she was launched on the Tyne on May 1934 and commissioned on November 6 for service with the 5th Destroyer Flotilla, Home Fleet. In the fall of 1939 she was fitted as a fast minelayer and allocated to the 20th Flotilla. In the early stages of the war, *Express* took part in several minelaying operations off the German North Sea coast, and in one off the coast of Norway. Between May 28 and June 3, 1940, she made six trips to Dunkirk, taking off a total of 3,500 soldiers, and was the second-last ship to leave the scene of the evacuation.

On August 31, 1940, *Express* and three other minelaying detroyers were preparing to lay mines off the coast of

▲ *(100)* **HMS Express**, *June 24, 1938. She became HMCS* **Gatineau** *in 1943.*

(101) **Gatineau** *in February 1945, just after completing a long refit at Halifax. Her newly-acquired Type 277 RDF was the first installed in an RCN ship.*

(102) **Gatineau** *at the gun wharf, Dartmouth, N.S., while refitting in August 1944.*

Holland near Texel when they blundered into a German minefield. *Esk* and *Ivanhoe* were sunk, while *Express* lost her entire bow. She was towed stern first to Hull, where in the course of the following year she received a new bow.

The ship now joined the 3rd Flotilla, sailing on October 25, 1941, as escort to HMS *Prince of Wales* to join the Eastern Fleet. She was present on the disastrous day of December 10, when *Prince of Wales* and *Repulse* were sunk by Japanese aircraft off Malaya, and rescued nearly 1,000 of *Prince of Wales'* ship's company. After serving with the Eastern Fleet throughout most of 1942, she returned to Britain to refit at Birkenhead.

On June 3, 1943, she was commissioned there as HMCS *Gatineau,* then proceeded to Tobermory for a month's workups. Allocated then to Escort Group C-2 as Senior Officer, she left Londonderry on July 2 to pick up her first convoy, ON.191. Owing to the setback suffered by the U-boats in May 1943, *Gatineau* enjoyed a fairly quiet time until September, when the combined convoy ON.202/ONS.18 became the object of renewed U-boat activity. Between September 20 and 23 the convoy was attacked by 20 U-boats, armed now with acoustic torpedoes. Only six of the 63 merchant vessels were lost, but three of the escorts were sunk and one damaged, one of those lost being HMCS *St. Croix.*

In December 1943 it was decided that C-2 should be employed for a time as a support group, and the last of nine convoys it assisted in this role was HX.280, early in March 1944. This convoy was attacked by a large group of U-boats, and late in the morning of March 5, *Gatineau* made contact with one of them. Thus began an attack by

(103) **Gatineau** *on the haul-out at Bay Bulls, Newfoundland, April 18, 1944. The sponsons to either side of her stern are a memento of her minelaying days.*

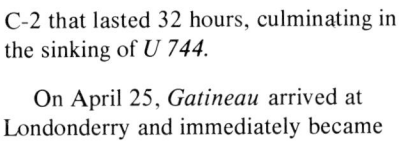

(104) and (105) Two views of **Gatineau** *in 1943.*

C-2 that lasted 32 hours, culminating in the sinking of *U 744*.

On April 25, *Gatineau* arrived at Londonderry and immediately became part of EG 11 with *Chaudière, Kootenay, Ottawa* and *St. Laurent*. From June 5 onward the group patrolled the west end of the Channel, to protect Normandy invasion traffic from U-boats. *Gatineau* left the group early in July, needing boiler repairs, and arrived at Halifax on the 29th for a long refit.

She did not return to U.K. waters until March 21, 1945, and then spent over a month working up at Tobermory before rejoining a reconstituted EG 11 (*Assiniboine, Kootenay* and *Saskatchewan*). The group continued its patrols through the last days of the war and for some weeks after, until all U-boats had been accounted for. They then returned to Canada after calling at Greenock, where a number of Canadian naval personnel were picked up for passage home.

Gatineau made two further trips to Greenock as a "troopship" before leaving Shelburne on August 10 for the west coast. It had been intended that she become a training ship for HMCS Royal Roads, but after carrying out an oceanographic project in November she was laid up and, on January 10, 1946, paid off. She was sold for scrap in 1946, and is officially stated to have been broken up later that year, but it is maintained in other circles that she was scuttled in 1948 as a breakwater at Royston, B.C.

			D/S DATE	GROUP, etc.	STATUS	D/S DATE	GROUP, etc	STATUS
						Dec. 7/43	EG C-2, MOEF	Repairs, Halifax
						Dec. 21/43	"	Left St. John's Dec. 19 for HX.271
						Jan. 11/44	"	U.K.
						Jan. 25/44	"	U.K.
						Feb. 8/44	"	U.K.
						Feb. 22/44	"	Supporting HX.279, Feb. 21
						Mar. 7/44	"	En route Moville March 6 from HX.280
						Mar. 21/44	"	U.K.
						Apr. 11/44	"	En route St. John's Apr. 10 from ON.230
						Apr. 25/44	"	Left St. John's Apr. 20 for Moville
						May 9/44	11th EG, CiC - WAC	Londonderry
			Apr. 14/43	-	U.K. port; to be ready for service June 28	May 23/44	"	Londonderry
			Apr. 27/43	-	"	June 6/44	"	Plymouth
			May 3/43	-	"	June 20/44	11th EG, CiC - Portsmouth	At sea
			May 13/43	-	"	July 4/44	"	At sea
			May 22/43	-	"	July 18/44	11th EG, CiC - Plymouth	Londonderry
			June 2/43	-	"	Aug. 8/44	"	Arr. Halifax July 29 for long refit
			June 12/43	-	"	Aug. 22/44	11th EG, CiC - WAC	Refitting, Halifax
			June 22/43	EG C-2, MOEF	Commissioned in U.K. June 3	Sep. 5/44	"	"
			July 6/43	"	Left U.K. July 1 c̄ ON.191	Sep. 19/44	"	"
			July 20/43	"	Leaving St. John's July 20 to join HX.248	Oct. 3/44	"	"
			Aug. 3/43	"	Arrived in U.K. from HX.248	Oct. 24/44	11th EG, CiC - Plymouth	"
			Aug. 17/43	"	Left U.K. Aug. 9 c̄ ON.196	Nov. 7/44	11th EG, CiC - WAC	"
			Sep. 7/43	"	U.K.	Nov. 21/44	"	"
			Sep. 21/43	"	Left Liverpool Sept. 16 with ON.202	Dec. 5/44	11th EG, CiC - NWAC	"
			Oct. 5/43	"	Repairs, St. John's	Dec. 19/44	"	"
			Oct. 19/43	"	Arrived in U.K. Oct. 13 from St. John's	Jan. 9/45	"	"
			Nov. 9/43	"	Arrived St. John's Nov. 2 from ONS.21	Jan. 23/45	"	"
			Nov. 23/43	"	Repairs, Halifax	Feb. 6/45	"	"

See note on p.102

GATINEAU

CHAUDIERE

Launched as HMS *Hero* on the Tyne on March 10, 1936, she joined the 2nd Destroyer Flotilla, Mediterranean Fleet, in 1937. In December 1939 she was detached to South Atlantic Station, but early in 1940 was recalled to join the 2nd Flotilla, Home Fleet. She was present at the second battle of Narvik on April 13, 1940.

The following month *Hero* returned to the Mediterranean, and on July 19 was part of a British squadron that sank two Italian cruisers off Cape Spada. Early in January 1941 she was one of the escort to an important Malta convoy code-named Operation "Excess". Late in April *Hero* took an active role in the evacuation of British troops from Greece, and in May was with the escort of another vital Malta convoy, Operation "Tiger". Later that month she took part in the evacuation of Crete. Toward the end of October she was near-missed by a bomb and slightly damaged while on a relief mission to Tobruk, and rescued survivors of HMS *Latona* when the latter was sunk on the same occasion.

Between March 20 and 22, 1942, *Hero* was part of the escort to Malta convoy MW.10, around which the second battle of Sirte developed and, though in action with the main Italian force, emerged unscathed. On May 28, with *Eridge* and *Hurworth,* she sank *U 568* off Sollum after a 15-hour hunt,

(106) *HMS Hero* in November 1936. She was to become HMCS *Chaudière* in 1943.

▶ (107) *Chaudière* on June 28, 1945 at Sydney, where she was paid off on August 17.

(108) Chaudière on August 16, 1944.

and on October 30 was one of a larger group that sank *U 559* northeast of Port Said. Again near-missed by a bomb in April 1943, *Hero* returned to the U.K. for a refit, following which she was transferred to the RCN and renamed *Chaudière*. She was commissioned at Portsmouth on November 15, 1943 and sailed for Scapa Flow a month later to work up.

Chaudière joined EG C-2 at Londonderry in mid-February, 1944, and was soon in the thick of the North Atlantic war. On March 5-6, as part of a support group assigned to convoy HX.280, she took part in the 32-hour "hunt to exhaustion" of what proved to be *U 744*. *Chaudière*'s boats rescued both the German survivors and the boarding parties of HMC ships *Chilliwack* and *St. Catharines*, whose boats had capsized against the surrendered *U 744*. It proved impractical to take the prize in tow, so HMS *Icarus,* the other destroyer present, sank her with a torpedo.

On April 25, *Chaudière* was assigned to a "hunter/killer" group of Canadian destroyers, the others being *Gatineau, Kootenay, Ottawa* (2nd) and *St. Laurent.* The group, EG 11, was to protect Normandy invasion traffic in the Channel, particularly from Biscay-based U-boats, and *Chaudière* distinguished herself in this employment, taking part in the destruction of three U-boats. On July 6, with *Ottawa* and HMS *Statice,* she sank *U 678* off Beachy Head, and on August 18 and 20, respectively, collaborated with *Ottawa* and *Kootenay* in the sinking of *U 621* and *U 984*.

In October, with the Channel stabilized, EG 11 was shifted to a patrol area south of Iceland, where it was anticipated that the dispossessed Biscay U-boats, now regrouped in Norway, might make a new start.

Poor weather on October 24 forced the group to seek shelter near Reykjavik, and that night *Skeena* dragged her anchors and was lost on the rocks. The others returned on November 5 to Londonderry, where *Chaudière, Qu'Appelle* and *St. Laurent* were ordered to proceed to Canada for refit. They worked their passage as escorts on convoy ON.267.

Chaudière began her refit at Sydney on January 22, 1945, but with some lack of urgency, as she had been adjudged to be in the poorest condition of all the remaining "Rivers". The European war ended on May 8, EG 11 was disbanded on June 6, and *Chaudière* declared surplus to requirements a week later. She was finally paid off on August 17 at Sydney and sold for scrap to Dominion Steel Company, who broke her up in 1950.

(109) and (110) Two views of **Chaudière**, *late in 1944.*

(111) *Chaudière* in February 1945, while refitting at Sydney. The photo provides a good view of the bridge arrangement, and of the ancient Hotchkiss guns to either side. Note also the Hedgehog mount immediately for'ard of the bridge.

D/S DATE	GROUP, etc.	STATUS	D/S DATE	GROUP, etc.	STATUS	D/S DATE	GROUP, etc.	STATUS
						Dec. 7/43	MOEF Unallocated	U.K., WUP
						Dec. 21/43	"	Left Portsmouth Dec. 17 for Scapa
						Jan. 11/44	EG C-2, MOEF	U.K.
						Jan. 25/44	"	U.K.
						Feb. 8/44	"	Arr. Londonderry Feb. 2 from Scapa
						Feb. 22/44	"	Supporting HX.279, Feb. 21
						Mar. 7/44	"	En route U.K. Mar. 6 from HX.280
						Mar. 21/44	"	U.K.
						Apr. 11/44	"	En route St. John's from ON.230, Apr. 10
						Apr. 25/44	"	Left St. John's Apr. 16 for HXF.287
						May 9/44	11th EG, CiC - WAC	Londonderry
						May 23/44	"	"
						June 6/44	"	Plymouth
						June 20/44	11th EG CiC - Portsmouth	At sea
						July 4/44	"	At sea
						July 18/44	11th EG CiC - Plymouth	Arr. Londonderry July 15 (?) from patrol
						Aug. 8/44	"	At sea
						Aug. 22/44	11th EG, CiC - WAC	Londonderry
						Sep. 5/44	"	At sea
						Sep. 19/44	"	At sea
						Oct. 3/44	"	At sea
						Oct. 24/44	11th EG CiC - Plymouth	At sea
						Nov. 7/44	11th EG, CiC - WAC	Arr. Londonderry Nov. 5 from Reykjavik
						Nov. 21/44	"	En route to ON.267 Nov. 20 from A/S search
						Dec. 5/44	11th EG, CiC - NWAC	Arr. Halifax Nov. 29 from ON.267
						Dec. 19/44	"	Repairs, Halifax
			Oct. 19/43	Ships being taken over from RN	Refitting, U.K.	Jan. 9/45	"	"
			Nov. 9/43	"	"	Jan. 23/45	"	Arr. Sydney Jan. 20 from Halifax
			Nov. 23/43	MOEF Unallocated	Commissioned Nov. 15	Feb. 6/45	"	Refitting, Sydney

See note on p.102

CHAUDIERE

QU'APPELLE

This ship was launched as HMS *Foxhound* in October 1934 and commissioned for service with the 6th Destroyer Flotilla, Home Fleet, on June 29, 1935. Between then and the outbreak of World War 2, the flotilla was predominantly engaged in patrolling the waters south and west of Spain as a result of the civil war there.

Foxhound and her sisters were based at Scapa Flow when the war began, and were assigned the task of patrolling the northern approaches to the North Sea. On September 14 she shared with *Faulknor* in the destruction of *U 49*, the first U-boat "kill" of the war. In April, 1940, *Foxhound* took part in the battle of Narvik, and in May escorted troopships involved in the occupation of Iceland. On her return she sailed with the Flotilla (renumbered as the 8th) to Gibraltar, where she became a member of the now-famous "Force H".

On July 3, it was *Foxhound* who carried Capt. C.S. Holland into Oran in a vain effort to win the French fleet there over to the Allies. At the end of the month she took part in Operation "Hurry", an air attack on Cagliari, Sicily, by aircraft from *Ark Royal*. On February she was present at the bombardment of Genoa, and on June 16, with three of her sisters, sank *U 138* near Gibraltar.

Early in 1942, *Foxhound* was transferred to the Eastern Fleet, with which she saw service in the Indian Ocean and Bay of Bengal before returning to the U.K. in mid-1943. Following a lengthy refit, she was commissioned as HMCS *Qu'Appelle* on February 8, 1944. At the time of her transfer, she had logged over 240,000 miles on war service.

After working up at Tobermory, *Qu'Appelle* briefly joined EG 6 at Londonderry, but in April was reassigned as Senior Officer to EG 12 with *Restigouche*, *Saguenay* and *Skeena*. From then until June 24 the group patrolled the west end of the Channel in support of invasion traffic, largely without incident. Their next patrol, early in July, was code-named Operation "Dredger", and was aimed at intercepting the armed trawlers that escorted U-boats in or out of Brest. In the course of this action *Qu'Appelle* suffered several casualties on the bridge, though none was fatal.

(112) HMS Foxhound, who became HMCS Qu'Appelle in 1944.

The group next undertook Operation "Kinetic", in which a German coastal convoy was attacked in Audierne Bay during the night of August 10/11. During the action, *Qu'Appelle* was struck on the starboard quarter by *Skeena*, and as a result was under repair until September 5. Escort Groups 11 and 12 were now amalgamated as EG 11, with *Qu'Appelle* still Senior Officer. The others were initially *Assiniboine, Chaudière, Ottawa* and *Restigouche,* but the latter two were shortly replaced by *Skeena* and *St. Laurent*. Their job was to counter an anticipated break-out into the Atlantic by U-boats now relocated in Norwegian bases.

After the storm in which *Skeena* was lost near Reykjavik, Oct. 24/25,

(113) HMS Foxhound in the Mediterranean, December 24, 1942.

(114) Qu'Appelle on April 16, 1944, escorting convoy ONM.231.

Qu'Appelle, Chaudière and *St. Laurent* proceeded to Canada for refit. *Qu'Appelle's* began at Halifax on December 5 and was completed at Pictou on June 30, 1945. The war being long over by then, she was assigned to the ferrying of service personnel home from the U.K., and made four crossings from Greenock before September 25. She was then transferred for training duty with the Torpedo School at HMCS Stadacona.

Qu'Appelle was paid off into reserve on May 26, 1946 and sold in December 1947 to German & Milne of Montreal, who broke her up in 1948.

(115) ***Qu'Appelle*** *at Londonderry in 1944.*

(116) ***Qu'Appelle*** *near the end of her days, stripped for disposal in 1945.*

			D/S DATE	GROUP, etc.	STATUS	D/S DATE	GROUP, etc.	STATUS
						Dec. 7/43	Ships being taken over from RN	Refitting in U.K.
						Dec. 21/43	"	"
						Jan. 11/44	"	"
						Jan. 25/44	"	"
						Feb. 8/44	"	Commissioned in U.K. Feb. 8
						Feb. 22/44	NWAC, unallocated	Tobermory, WUP
						Mar. 7/44	"	"
						Mar. 21/44	6th EG, CiC - WAC	At sea on A/S patrol
						Apr. 11/44	"	Left U.K. Apr. 8 c̄ ONM.231
						Apr. 25/44	"	Left St. John's Apr. 23 for Londonderry
						May 9/44	12th EG, CiC - WAC	Londonderry
						May 23/44	12th EG, RCN	"
						June 6/44	" (S.O.)	Plymouth
						June 20/44	" (S.O.)	At sea
						July 4/44	" (S.O.)	At sea
						July 18/44	" (S.O.)	At sea
						Aug. 8/44	" (S.O.)	Londonderry
						Aug. 22/44	12th EG, CiC - WAC (S.O.)	Plymouth
						Sep. 5/44	"	"
						Sep. 19/44	11th EG, CiC - WAC	At sea
						Oct. 3/44	"	At sea
						Oct. 24/44	11th EG CiC - Plymouth	At sea
						Nov. 7/44	11th EG CiC - WAC (S.O.)	Arr. Londonderry Nov. 5 from Reykjavik
						Nov. 21/44	"	En route to ON.267, Nov. 20 from A/S search
						Dec. 5/44	11th EG, CiC - NWAC (S.O.)	Arr. Halifax Nov. 29 from ON.267
						Dec. 19/44	"	Repairs, Halifax
				Oct. 19/43	Ships being taken over from RN	Refitting in U.K.	Jan. 9/45	"	Refitting, Pictou
				Nov. 9/43	"	"	Jan. 23/45	"	"
				Nov. 23/43	"	"	Feb. 6/45	"	"

See note on p.102

QU'APPELLE

ENVOI...

(117) Two "Rivers" looking a trifle ill at ease among a group of newer, larger consorts. At Halifax on September 23, 1945 (l-r): Saskatchewan, Micmac, St. Laurent, Huron and Sioux.

GENERAL NOTES

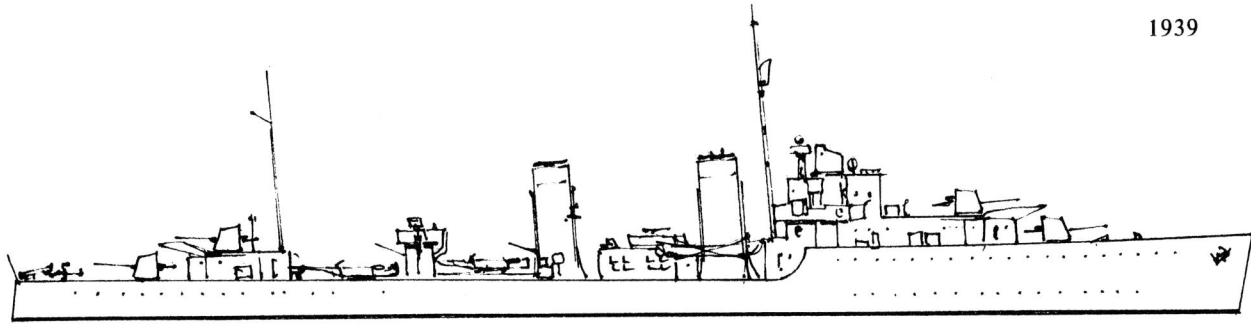

1939

While it seems virtually impossible now to detail and date the modifications made in adapting each of these ships for escort work, the following sequence of events may be considered typical:

Main Armament

The original armament of four 4.7" guns had been reduced to two or three by the end of the war. In 1942 all members of the class lost "Y" turret to make room for the additional depth charge throwers and chutes that made possible a ten-charge pattern. In 1943 some lost "B" turret as well, to make room for a Hedgehog mounting, while others received a "split" Hedgehog and thus were able to retain "B" gun.

Secondary Armament

The 2-pounder pompoms at first located to either side between the funnels were replaced in 1940 by quadruple .5" machine guns. These in their turn gave place to 20mm weapons (Oerlikons) in 1942, two more of the latter appearing on the bridge wings and a further two on the erstwhile searchlight platform.

A 12-pounder anti-aircraft gun replaced the after torpedo tube mounting in 1940, but this was removed about 1942 in most cases to make room for extra depth charge stowage. The newly installed 20mm guns had in any case usurped its function.

Torpedo tubes

As noted, the after set of four was removed in 1940, depth charge and A.A. armament being of more use in convoy escort work. The customary load in the remaining four tubes was two Mk. IX torpedoes and two Mk.X depth charges.

RDF (Radar)

The first RDF fitted (about 1941) was Type 286, whose antenna resembled a rudimentary bedspring at the foremast head, and by most accounts was about as useful. This was replaced late in 1942 by Type 271, whose familiar "lantern" supplanted the director control tower and rangefinder atop the wheelhouse.

General

The mainmast, struck in 1940 to give a wider arc of fire to the 3" gun, reappeared late in 1942 in lattice form, topped by the "bird cage" antenna of the HF/DF set. In 1941 the after funnel was shortened by some seven feet, presumably to decrease top weight.

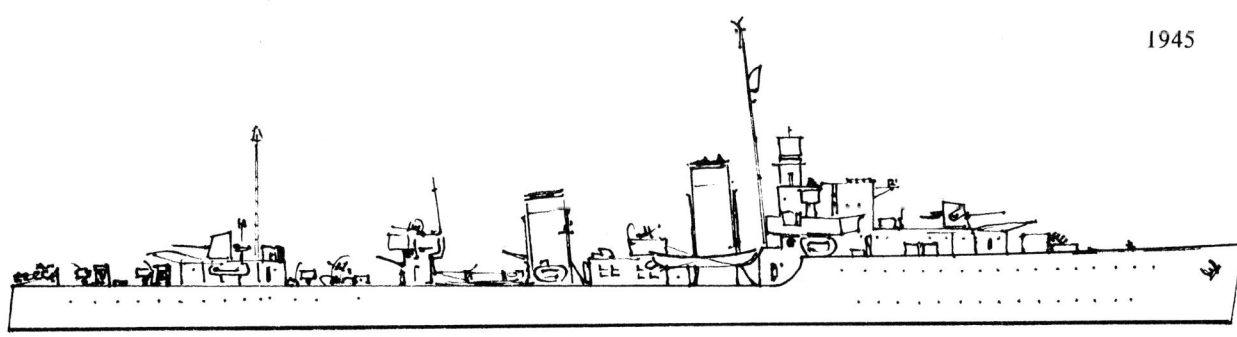

1945

INTERNAL ARRANGEMENT

NOTE: The drawing is a greatly simplified version of one by Samuel White & Co. of HMS *Kempenfelt*, dated June 16, 1932. This ship became HMCS *Assiniboine* in October 1939, and the general arrangements are essentially the same for all River class units. By the time she was acquired by the RCN the whaler and motor cutter had exchanged places, and the 2-pounder guns on the fo'c'sle deck had been re-sited between the funnels in place of the 3" H.A.

1. Tiller flat
2. Officers' cabins (P & S)
3. Wardroom
4. X.O.'s cabin (P), Wardroom pantry (S)
5. Officer's cabin (P), Captain's pantry (S)
6. C.O.'s sleeping cabin (P) and day cabin (S)
7. Officers' cabins (P & S), switchboard room amidships
8. Spirit room
9. C.O.'s and wardroom stores (P)
10. 4.7" magazine and shellroom
11. Torpedo head magazine
12. Fuel tank
13. Engine room
14. After boiler room
15. Forward boiler room
16. Main W/T office
17. Fire control wireless office
18. Transmitting station
19. Seamen's mess
20. Paint locker
21. Low power supply room (P), crew space (S)
22. Stoker P.O.'s mess (P)
23. E.R.A.'s mess (P), stewards' mess (S)
24. Stokers' mess

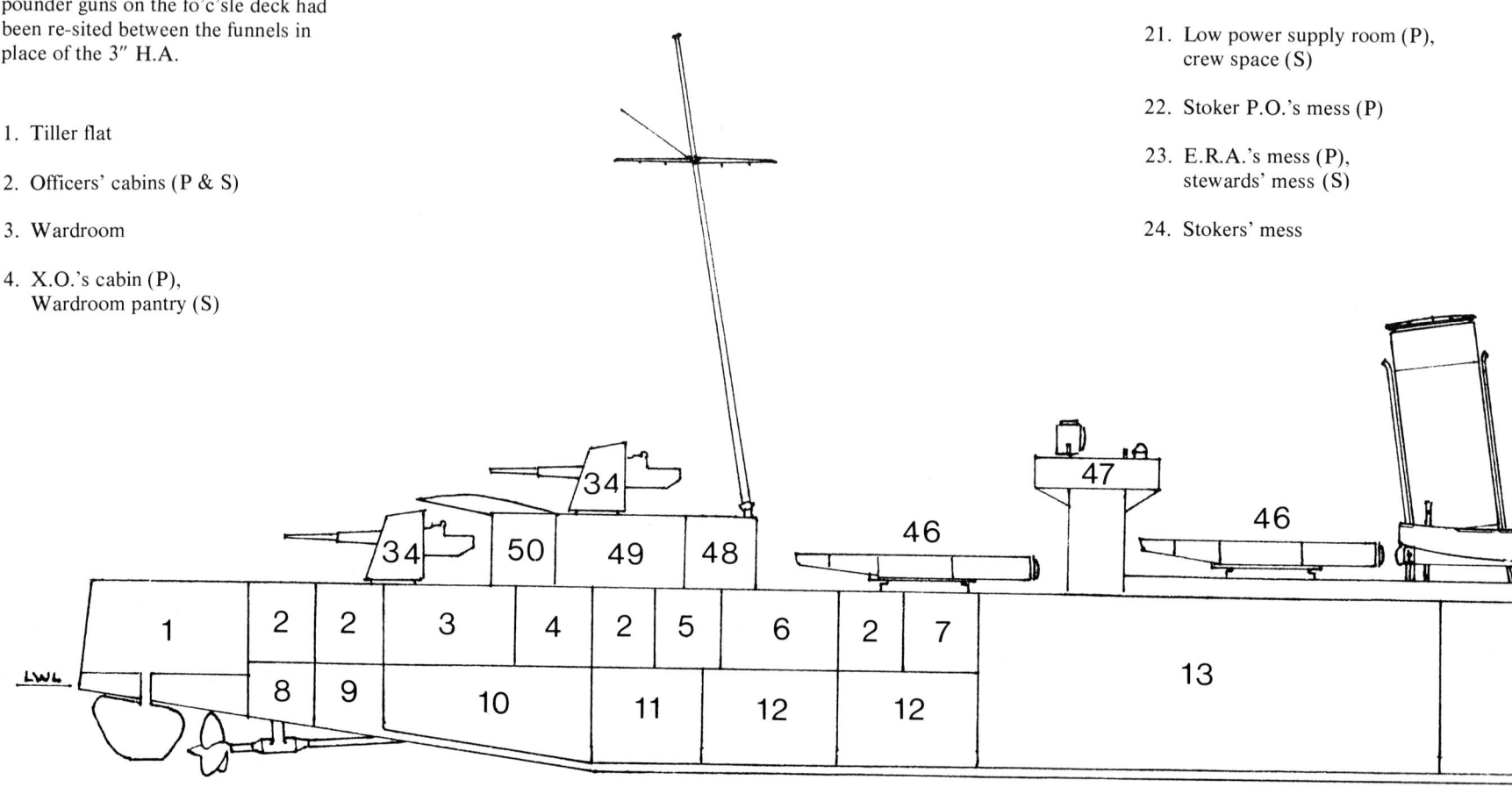

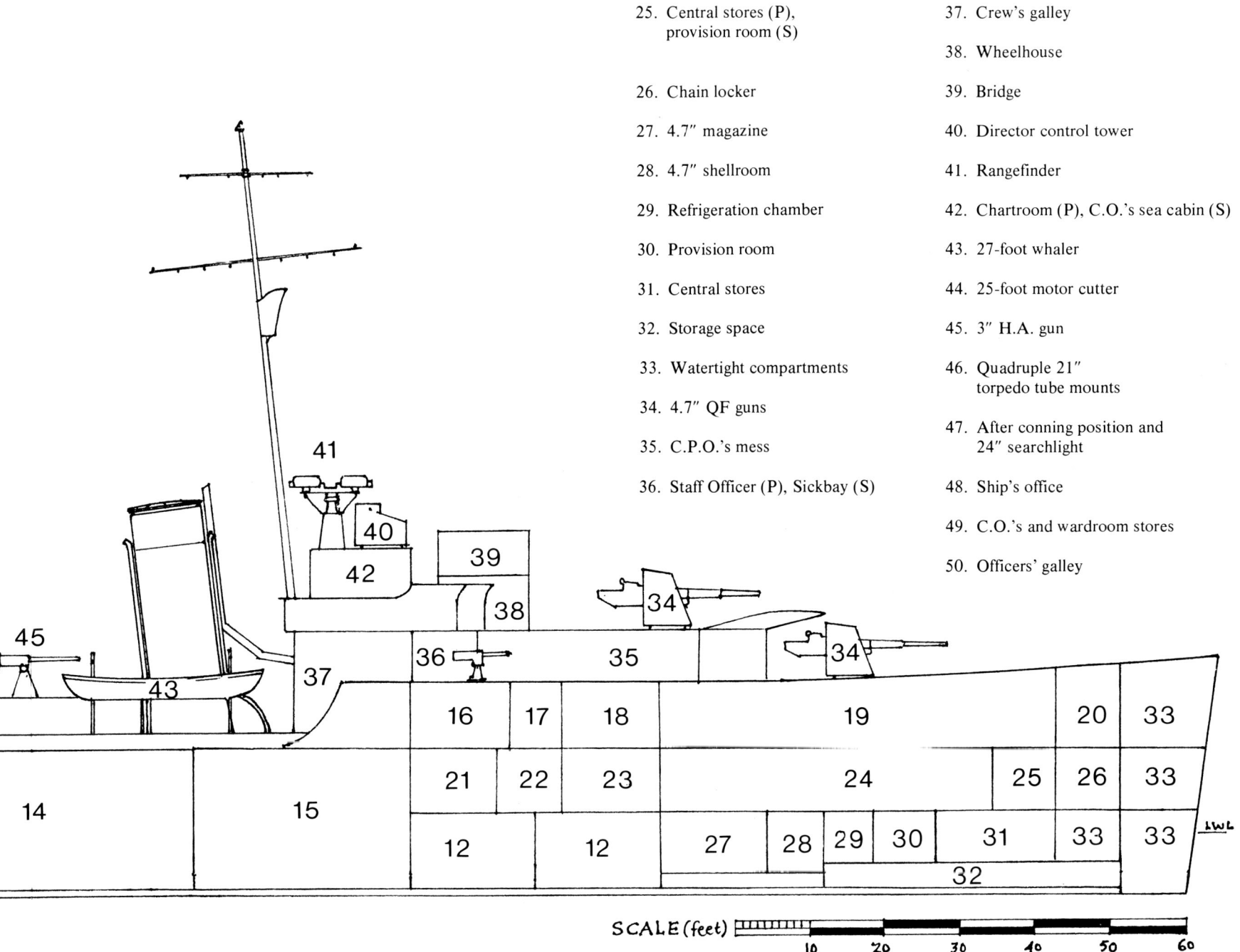

25. Central stores (P), provision room (S)
26. Chain locker
27. 4.7″ magazine
28. 4.7″ shellroom
29. Refrigeration chamber
30. Provision room
31. Central stores
32. Storage space
33. Watertight compartments
34. 4.7″ QF guns
35. C.P.O.'s mess
36. Staff Officer (P), Sickbay (S)
37. Crew's galley
38. Wheelhouse
39. Bridge
40. Director control tower
41. Rangefinder
42. Chartroom (P), C.O.'s sea cabin (S)
43. 27-foot whaler
44. 25-foot motor cutter
45. 3″ H.A. gun
46. Quadruple 21″ torpedo tube mounts
47. After conning position and 24″ searchlight
48. Ship's office
49. C.O.'s and wardroom stores
50. Officers' galley

Ship's Name/Builder	No.	a. Laid Down b. Launched c. Comm. in RCN d. Paid Off	Displ. (tons)	a. Length b. Breadth C. Draught	Armament (As acquired/final)
SAGUENAY Thornycroft Ltd., Southampton, England	D/I79	a. Sept. 27, 1929 b. July 11, 1930 c. May 22, 1931 d. July 30, 1945	1,337	a. 320' b. 32'6" c. 10'	4-4.7", 2-2 pdrs., 8-21" TT (2 x IV) 2-4.7", 1-3" H.A., 4-20mm, 4-21" TT, Hedgehog
SKEENA Thornycroft Ltd., Southampton, England	D/I59	a. Oct. 14, 1929 b. Oct. 10, 1930 c. June 10, 1931 d. Oct. 25, 1944	1,337	a. 320' b. 32'6" c. 10'	4-4.7", 2-2 pdrs., 8-21" TT (2 x IV) 2-4.7", 1-3" H.A., 4-20mm, 4-21" TT, Hedgehog
FRASER **(ex-CRESCENT)** Vickers-Armstrong Ltd., Barrow-in-Furness, Eng.	H48	a. Feb. 1, 1930 b. Sept. 29, 1931 c. Feb. 17, 1937 d. June 28, 1940	1,375	a. 329' b. 33' c. 10'2"	4-4.7", 2-2 pdrs., 8-21" TT (2 x IV) 4-4.7", 1-3" H.A., 2-2 pdrs., 4-21" TT
ST. LAURENT **(ex-CYGNET)** Vickers-Armstrong Ltd., Barrow-in-Furness, Eng.	H83	a. Dec. 1, 1930 b. Sept. 29, 1931 c. Feb. 17, 1937 d. Oct. 10, 1945	1,375	a. 329' b. 33' c. 10'2"	4-4.7", 2-2 pdrs., 8-21" TT (2 x IV) 2-4.7", 6-20mm, 4-21" TT, Hedgehog
OTTAWA **(ex-CRUSADER)** Portsmouth Dockyard, Eng.	H60	a. Sept. 12, 1930 b. Sept. 30, 1931 c. June 15, 1938 d. Sept. 14, 1942	1,375	a. 329' b. 33' c. 10'2"	4-4.7", 2-2 pdrs., 8-21" TT (2 x IV) 3-4.7", 1-3" H.A., 2-20mm, 4-21" TT.
RESTIGOUCHE **(ex-COMET)** Portsmouth Dockyard, Eng.	H00	a. Sept. 12, 1930 b. Sept. 30, 1931 c. June 15, 1938 d. Oct. 6, 1945	1,375	a. 329' b. 33' c. 10'2"	4-4.7", 2-2 pdrs., 8-21" TT (2 x IV) 2-4.7", 6-20mm, 2-6 pdr. Hotchkiss, Hedgehog
ASSINIBOINE **(ex-KEMPENFELT)** J. Samuel White & Co., Cowes, Isle of Wight	D/I18	a. Oct. 18, 1930 b. Oct. 29, 1931 c. Oct. 19, 1939 d. Aug. 8, 1945	1,390	a. 329' b. 33' c. 10'6"	4-4.7", 2-2 pdrs., 8-21" TT (2 x IV) 3-4.7", 6-20mm, 4-21" TT, Hedgehog
MARGAREE **(ex-DIANA)**	H49	a. June 12, 1931 b. June 16, 1932 c. Sept. 6, 1940 d. Oct. 22, 1940	1,375	a. 329' b. 33' c. 10'2"	4-4.7", 1-3" H.A., 2-quadruple .5" m.g., 4-21" TT (2 x IV)

Ship's Name/Builder	No.	a. Laid Down b. Launched c. Comm. in RCN d. Paid Off	Displ. (tons)	a. Length b. Breadth c. Draught	Armament (As acquired/final)
OTTAWA (2nd) **(ex-GRIFFIN)** Vickers-Armstrong Ltd., Barrow-in-Furness, Eng.	H31	a. Sept. 20, 1934 b. Aug. 15, 1935 c. Mar. 20, 1943 d. Oct. 31, 1945	1,335	a. 323' b. 33' c. 10'7"	4-4.7", 1-3" H.A., 2-quadruple .5" m.g., 8-21" TT (2 x IV) 2-4.7", 6-20mm, 4-21" TT, Hedgehog
KOOTENAY **(ex-DECOY)** Thornycroft Ltd., Southampton, England	H75	a. June 25, 1931 b. June 7, 1932 c. Apr. 12, 1943 d. Oct. 26, 1945	1,375	a. 329' b. 33'3" c. 10'2"	4-4.7", 1-3" H.A., 2-quadruple .5" m.g., 8-21" TT (2 x IV) 3-4.7", 7-20mm, 4-21" TT, Hedgehog
SASKATCHEWAN **(ex-FORTUNE)** John Brown & Co., Clydebank, Scotland	H70	a. July 25, 1933 b. Aug. 29, 1934 c. May 31, 1943 d. Jan. 28, 1946	1,405	a. 329' b. 33'3" c. 10'10"	3-4.7", 1-3" H.A., 8-21" TT (2 x IV) 3-4.7", 6-20mm, 4-21" TT, Hedgehog
GATINEAU **(ex-EXPRESS)** Swan, Hunter Ltd., Wallsend-on-Tyne, Eng.	H61	a. Mar. 23, 1933 b. May 29, 1934 c. June 3, 1943 d. Jan. 10, 1946	1,375	a. 329' b. 33'3" c. 10'10"	4-4.7", 1-3" H.A., 2-quadruple .5" m.g., 8-21" TT (2 x IV) 3-4.7", 6-20mm, 4-21" TT, Hedgehog
CHAUDIERE **(ex-HERO)** Vickers-Armstrong Ltd., Newcastle-on-Tyne, Eng.	H99	a. Feb. 28, 1935 b. Mar. 10, 1936 c. Nov. 15, 1943 d. Aug. 17, 1945	1,350	a. 329' b. 33' c. 9'11"	2-4.7", 6-20mm, 2-6 pdr. Hotchkiss, 4-21" TT (2 x IV), Hedgehog
QU'APPELLE **(ex-FOXHOUND)** John Brown & Co., Clydebank, Scotland	H69	a. Aug. 21, 1933 b. Oct. 12, 1934 c. Feb. 8, 1944 d. May 27, 1946	1,405	a. 329' b. 33'3" c. 10'10"	2-4.7", 6-20mm, 2-6 pdr. Hotchkiss, 4-21" TT (2 x IV), Hedgehog

NOTE: The early war complement of these ships was typically 7 officers, 160 other ranks. By war's end this had risen on average to 13 officers, 182 other ranks. Effective top speed was about 31 knots.

The 6-pounders installed in *Chaudière* and *Qu'Appelle* were located in "B" gun deck to either side of the bridge. In *Chaudière's* case, at least, they were removed in 1944. *Ottawa* (2nd) and *Saskatchewan* sported 2-pounder bow chasers for a time, but these proved useless and were removed late in 1944.

EXPLANATORY NOTES

The operational status charts that appear at the end of each ship's narrative were compiled by John Burgess in the course of assembling material for our joint work, The Ships of Canada's Naval Forces, 1910-1981. Sad to relate, the Daily and Weekly State reports upon which they are based appear not to have survived for the period before February 27, 1942, and after February 6, 1945. This explains, not only the abbreviated nature of the charts, but the fact that *Fraser's* and *Margaree's* narratives lack them. Both ships were lost prior to the period for which information is available.

References to convoys and escort groups are frequent in the book, and a word of explanation may be useful:

Eastbound convoys were designated "HX" or "SC". The former sailed at first from Halifax to the U.K. and (beginning in September 1942) from New York. The latter originated first at Sydney, N.S., later at Halifax, and later still at New York. HX convoys were "fast", SC convoys "slow"; meaning, in practical terms, 9 and 7½ knots respectively. Westbound convoys, similarly, were designated "ON" and "ONS" — the former fast, the latter slow.

The escort groups to which these ships belonged were officially designated C-1 to C-5 (C denoting "Canadian") in April 1943, after being so known unofficially for the better part of a year.

A typical escort group might consist of two or three destroyers and five or six corvettes (later frigates), but they were chronically under strength owing to members under refit or repair. Escort Groups 11 and 12, to which all the remaining Rivers were assigned in May 1944, were "support groups", which functioned independently of the convoy cycle but were used, among other things, to bolster the escort of beleaguered convoys when required. A major function was that of patrolling the Western Approaches to the English Channel during and after D Day.

Abbreviations used in the book are as follows:

A/A	Anti-Aircraft
A/S	Anti-Submarine
CiC	Commander-in-Chief
EG	Escort Group
H.A.	High Angle
H/F D/F	High-Frequency Direction-Finding
JH	St. John's-Halifax convoy
MOEF	Mid-Ocean Escort Force
NOIC	Naval Officer in Charge
NWAC	North West Atlantic Command
RDF	Radio Direction Finder (Radar)
S.O.	Senior Officer's Ship
TT	Torpedo Tubes
WAC	Western Approaches Command
W/T	Wireless Telegraphy (Radio)
WUP	Working Up

SELECTED BIBLIOGRAPHY

Easton, Alan *50 North: an Atlantic Battleground*. London: Eyre & Spottiswoode, 1963.

Lenton, H.T. *British Fleet and Escort Destroyers,* vol. 1. London: Macdonald, 1970.

Macintyre, Donald *The Battle of the Atlantic.* London: Batsford, 1961.

Macpherson, Ken *Canada's Fighting Ships.* Toronto: Samuel Stevens, 1975.

Macpherson, Ken and Burgess, John *The Ships of Canada's Naval Forces, 1910-1981.* Toronto: Collins, 1981.

March, Edgar J. *British Destroyers: a History of Development, 1892-1953.* London: Sealey Services & Co., Ltd., 1966.

Morison, Samuel Eliot *History of the United States Naval Operations in World War II,* I, *The Battle of the Atlantic, September 1939-May 1943.* Boston: Little, Brown, 1947; and X, *The Atlantic Battle Won, May 1943-May 1945.* Boston: Little, Brown, 1956.

Rayner, D.A. Escort: *the Battle of the Atlantic.* London: William Kimber, 1955.

Roskill, Stephen W. *The War at Sea, 1939-1945* (4 vols.). London: H.M. Stationery Office, 1954-1961,

Schull, Joseph. *The Far Distant Ships.* Ottawa: D.N.D., 1952.

Tucker, Gilbert N. *The Naval Service of Canada, Its Official History* (2 vols.) Ottawa: D.N.D., 1952.

PHOTO CREDITS

Most of the photographs used in this book are held by Public Archives of Canada, whose negative numbers, where known, are listed below. The rest are from other institutions and from private individuals, whom I have done my best to acknowledge.

2. PAC CN.3071
3. Rupert McMichael
4. James Plomer
6. PAC NF.14
7. PAC CN.3531
8. RCAF
9. PAC NF.1249
10. RCAF
11. B.A. Earthy
12. Hayward Photo
13. PAC PMR 73-146
14. Ken Kelley
15. PAC N.9
16. PAC N.16
17. PAC N.1
18. PAC H.2317A
19. PAC HS.0487-9
20. R.A. Broomer
21. PAC HN.1842
22. PAC CN.3168
23. PAC E.2290
24. PAC E.2294
25. RCAF
26. PAC CN.3804
27. James Plomer
28. Keystone
29. Cribb, Southsea
30. James Plomer
31. James Plomer
32. PAC H.1848
33. PAC CN.6248
34. PAC HS.0284-5
35. C. VanLaughton
36. PAC A.1566
37. Stephen Burd
38. N. Coombe
39. Cribb, Southsea
40. James Plomer
41. PAC H.200
42. PAC H.206
45. A.G.S. Griffin
46. PAC N.186
47. PAC NF.532
48. PAC H.2239
49. PAC NF.979
50. B.A. Earthy
51. PAC NF.980
52. A. Pavia
53. PAC N.11
54. PAC H.538
55. PAC H.539
56. PAC NP.489
57. PAC NP.607
58. Imperial War Museum
60. PAC H.749
61. PAC H.747
62. PAC H.306
63. PAC NF.401
64. W.S. Knapp
65. PAC NF.781
66. PAC NF.785
67. PAC H.3093
68. PAC O.1794
69. W. McMullen
70. PAC CN.6261
72. PAC CN.6235
73. Admiralty, U.K.
75. Abrahams, Devonport
76. PAC A.102
77. PAC HS.0239-9
78. PAC HS.0239-4
79. PAC R.166
80. PAC A.101
81. David Brindle
82. PAC L.4125
83. PAC L.4124
85. R.A. Broomer
86. E.G. Giles
89. PAC A.1010
90. Admiralty, U.K.
91. PAC HS.0343-65
92. PAC O-6154
93. John Small
94. A. Nelson
95. A. Nelson
96. PAC HS.0343-66
97. PAC Z.990
98. PAC SY.161-16
100. Wright & Logan
101. PAC S.3311
102. PAC S.1609
103. PAC NF.3611-3
104. PAC
106. R. Perkins
107. PAC SY.161-7
108. PAC A.1004
109. RCAF
111. PAC HS.0940-10
112. PAC CN.6677
113. Admiralty, U.K.
114. RCAF
116. PAC HS.0343-80
117. Author's photo